MIDLAND CITY:

RECOVERING PROSPERITY THROUGH QUALITY

MIDLAND CITY:

RECOVERING PROSPERITY THROUGH QUALITY

ROBERT A. SCHWARZ

ASQC QUALITY PRESS

42255

MIDLAND CITY: RECOVERING PROSPERITY THROUGH QUALITY

ROBERT A. SCHWARZ

Acquisitions Editor: Jeanine L. Lau
Production Editor: Tammy Griffin
Cover Design: Artistic License
Set in Century Schoolbook by DanTon Typographers.
Printed and bound by Edwards Brothers.

Published by ASQC Quality Press • Milwaukee

ASQC Quality Press
American Society for Quality Control
310 West Wisconsin Avenue, Milwaukee, Wisconsin 53203

ISBN 0-87389-052-3

10987654321

Printed in the United States of America

Contents

Preface vii

Acknowledgments ix

Chapter 1 The Letter 1
Chapter 2 A Time of Terror: Four Years Earlier 5
Chapter 3 The Vision 7
Chapter 4 The Town Meeting 11
Chapter 5 The Costs of Nonquality 20
Chapter 6 The Manufacturers 23
Chapter 7 The Talk 26
Chapter 8 The Strategic Planning Meeting 28
Chapter 9 The Suggestion System 35
Chapter 10 Training 40
Chapter 11 Midland City Schools 45
Chapter 12 Scott's Project 55
Chapter 13 Midland City Fulfillment: Work Flow
Analysis/Work Simplification 58
Chapter 14 Midland City Machine: Value Analysis 71
Chapter 15 Midland City Motors 78
Chapter 16 Local Merchants 85
Chapter 17 Trock Plastics: Design of Experiments 88
Chapter 18 Thirty Months 93
Chapter 19 Japan: Just-in-Time and Total Quality Control 99
Chapter 20 The Lead 107
Chapter 21 Reaching Out 109

Appendices 113

Team Problem Solving/Quality Circles 114
Suggestion Systems 135
Nominal Group Technique 161
Process Summary Charts 166
Measuring Performance 177
Performance Improvement Process 185
Glossary 187

Preface

Midland City is a typical rural community located somewhere in America. The city has lost much of its population base through consolidation of farms. It has lost jobs in the city and is facing a steadily declining economy. In short, either something happens or the city will gradually die.

This book was written to provide a vision of how a community can shape its destiny and how it can cause the changes that would bring in new jobs and growth.

I wrote *Midland City* as a novel to place characters with names and accomplishments in a context. I felt a book could show how each person in the city must learn new skills in working together and solving problems. We need a vision of both the result and the parts that lead to the result.

This book is designed to bring an acceptance of change by everyone in the community as well as to provide a "how to" on the methods and processes for change. Have fun reading and even more fun changing your city.

Change is here. Either we manage it or it manages us.

ROBERT A. "BOB" SCHWARZ created the manuscript for *Midland City* in the form of a novel to help create a vision of how quality can be improved. Born in Paynesville, Minnesota, Bob has lived in a number of other rural communities. He serves as a director on two state-wide boards for vocational education and as a participant on many committees for productivity and quality improvement. He has been published in magazines and has lectured at numerous conferences.

Formerly an employee of Honeywell Inc., Bob is presently president of Total Quality Systems, located in Minneapolis. He has a degree in mechanical engineering and extensive training in a wide range of productivity processes. He is past national president for the American Society for Performance Improvement, director of the Minnesota Consortium for Quality and Productivity, and a member of the American Society for Quality Control.

The original manuscript was edited by **SHELLY BEAUDRY.** Shelly has a strong background in newspaper reporting with a focus on business, educational, and local government issues. She has a bachelor of arts degree in newspaper journalism and speech communication from the University of Minnesota.

Together, Bob and Shelly have written a book that creates a compelling vision. Influenced by the effective motivation and leadership of a quality system, your community could benefit from the same success as "Midland City."

Acknowledgments

Midland City involved many good friends. They deserve credit for ensuring the accuracy of the examples used in the various chapters. Because of their help, I can be assured that the changes described are all possible. I wanted *Midland City* to be both a source of a vision and a "how to" book providing details.

My thanks to Radcliffe "Buck" Ashworth, Hennepin County; Lou Mikunda, Honeywell Inc.; John Robertson, Extensor Corp.; Clint Soppeland, Honeywell Inc.; Roger Syverson, Professional Value Services; and Ted Tammearu, Honeywell Inc. for their review of technologies.

Thanks also to my wife, Gloria, for her continuous review support during preparation.

CHAPTER 1

The Letter

It was the best day he'd had in the six years he had been mayor of Midland City, Bill Peterson thought as he rested his feet on the top of his desk. It was a day to celebrate, yet he couldn't feel too relaxed. He and his community still had a lot of work to do.

Earlier in the day just about everyone in Midland City, young and old, had celebrated at Bingle Park. The high school band played, and the City Quality Program supplied free bratwurst, lemonade, and ice cream for everyone. Bill had proudly unveiled the new signs for the highway leading to Midland City. The signs, stressing the city's pride and dedication to quality, would be posted along with the signs featuring the Midland City Cougars' victory in the 1984 State Boys Basketball Championship.

Even Lieutenant Governor Betty Graham and three state legislators were at the park to share in the celebration. Apex Corporation had chosen Midland City, a city of 8,216, as the location for its new electronics plant.

It was a tough fight — plenty of mayors had attempted to lure the Apex plant to their cities, along with the 400 to 600 jobs it would create. But Apex opted for Midland City. Alan Kotch, president of Apex, said it was because Midland City was a fine community where he would be proud to bring his family and one where his company could prosper.

WELCOME TO MIDLAND CITY

8,216 PEOPLE DEDICATED TO QUALITY

THE BEST SCHOOLS IN THE STATE

SIX OUTSTANDING CORPORATIONS

THE BEST SERVICE AND QUALITY FROM OUR
MERCHANTS AND RESTAURANTS

STOP AND SEE FOR YOURSELF

WELCOME TO MIDLAND CITY

HOME OF THE COUGARS

1984 STATE BOYS BASKETBALL

CHAMPIONS

Four years earlier Apex wouldn't have even considered the community in which Bill was born and then went on to raise his own family. The thought churned his stomach. At that time Midland City was quietly dying. Sure he and his administrators had put out fires, sobered up drunks, and filled potholes, but the problems weren't so much in appearances as they were in attitudes, economics, and, as much as he hated to admit, leadership.

Even his wife, Samantha, had tried to talk him into packing up and moving their son and daughter to the suburbs of Meadan, the state's thriving capital city. "It has an excellent school system where the teachers really seem to care," she had told Bill. "And you could find a job easily. After all, my father is city manager there."

But Bill couldn't leave his hometown of 42 years — not in the shape it was in. Parents, unhappy with the public school system, were transferring their children to St. Paul's Elementary School. Some parents with older children were moving to other communities with better schools. Midland City Bank was foreclosing on numerous farms, businesses on Main Street were closing their doors, and people were either moving to larger cities or living on less income.

Bill knew it was up to him to do something. After all, his late father, Dale Peterson, had been mayor of Midland City 30 years before. Bill wasn't about to let his father's dream die — a dream that Midland City would once again flourish.

And he hadn't, he thought proudly as the telephone rang. It was Samantha.

"Hi, Sam," Bill said to his wife of 20 years. At 40 she was as beautiful as the day he married her, he thought fondly.

"When are you coming home?" she asked. "I just got home from picking Scott up from hockey practice, and Sarah just finished cooking dinner. We're waiting for you."

Bill hadn't realized it was already 6:30 p.m. Had he been daydreaming that long?

"I'm sorry, honey. I didn't know it was so late. I was just reviewing the letter from Alan Kotch, the president of Apex. And you know what? He wrote that it's an honor to locate his plant here."

"That's wonderful Bill," Samantha said sincerely. She wondered why she had ever questioned sticking it out in Midland City. At times Bill had been almost unbearable to live with, and often all he could think about was Midland City. But he was dedicated to something he believed in, and she believed in him.

"Can I expect you soon?" she asked.

"Sure. I'll leave as soon as I read Kotch's letter one more time."

In his letter Kotch explained at great length why his company had selected Midland City. He complimented those people who had worked so hard to rebuild the city. The planning, meetings, and hard work had really paid off, Peterson thought to himself as he read on:

The Midland City school system has become one of the best in the state. Its SAT scores and other records of academic achievement, not to mention its athletic programs, are envied by the best schools.

This kind of school performance will draw key technical and management staff with families. And the fact that the school district's curriculum emphasizes statistics and team problem solving assures me that new hires for Apex will be better prepared for our complex challenges.

I commend Midland City School Superintendent Helen Sikorski for her work.

Apex looks forward to hiring many of the fine graduates of your outstanding nearby technical institute and junior college. We at Apex feel the people of Midland City can outperform workers anywhere. They reflect both excellent training and a work-quality attitude unmatched by the other cities we reviewed. We're confident we will not have to spend much time and money training people to do a quality job.

We plan to allow job sharing and offer some seasonal work opportunities for area farmers — a benefit we hope will help keep many of them in business.

Midland's reputation as a "Community of Quality" will greatly benefit Apex when our representatives approach new customers. I respect the way everyone in Midland City has worked together to make theirs the best city in the state, especially how Midland City manufacturers share ideas on how to better manage their plants.

It's impressive how your city established the funds to hire consultants and send 10 representatives to Japan to study its manufacturers' management strategies.

Apex is proud to take part in Midland City's quest for quality. We are looking forward only to success.

Bill liked the attention the media had given him at the picnic that day, he thought as he carefully tucked the letter into his briefcase. Not just any mayor is asked to pose repeatedly for photos with the lieutenant governor. And there had been rumors about his successfully vying for the soon-to-be-open senate seat in his district. Why not? Hadn't he provided the vital leadership for his friends?

Bill felt good about being a winner.

CHAPTER 2

A Time of Terror: Four Years Earlier

The call came at about 10:30 on a Friday morning. Bill Peterson had just finished nine holes of golf at the municipal course with Ralph Huber, mayor of Rainville. They played every Friday.

The day had started out badly. He double bogied the first hole, tore up the fairway on the last hole, and finished his game with an embarrassing 50, well above his normal four handicap. And after hearing the tone of the police chief's voice, he knew things weren't going to get much better.

"There's been a shooting out at the Braddock farm," said Midland Police Chief Spetch, as he struggled to catch his breath.

Joe Braddock hadn't made a loan payment in many months. Carl Randall, Midland City bank president, had covered up the delinquent payments as long as he could, but the bank board finally voted to foreclose on Joe's farm.

Joe and his family were devastated by the foreclosure, but Bill never dreamed Joe would resort to such desperate measures. Maybe he would have done something too, if his family's livelihood was at stake.

"Randall and the auctioneer both were wounded and have been taken to Midland City Hospital. We have Joe down here at the city jail," Spetch said.

"I'll be right there," Bill said as he grabbed his coat.

A new auctioneer was brought in. By late afternoon Braddock's possessions were sold and the eviction was completed.

A pall of near death hung over Midland City like a thick wet fog enveloping everything in a state of confusion and frustration. No one seemed to know what to do or where to turn.

People they had known all of their lives were turning frustration into violence — a far different breed of violence than the type their beloved

Cougars exhibited when they wiped out their opponents on the football field the previous Friday.

Unfortunately, the Braddock sale and foreclosure were typical of the actions that seemed to be happening monthly. The farmers' products brought a return that barely covered the cost of seed, fuel, and chemicals. Their massive debt was the result of an unfavorable national policy coupled with an economy that had disastrously lured many of them to mortgage their precious land to buy machinery. Some farmers blamed the federal government — an entity that seemed much too distant and foreign to bring their troubles. So they directed their anger at the local banker.

But the banker had to minimize his risk. Without payments he could lose his bank. As much as he tried to tell his side of the story, he still became the "bad guy" — a proverbial catch-22.

Main Street also had its problems. Farmers, its mainstay, were cash poor so each local business sold fewer products and, in turn, had fewer dollars to generate back into the economy. Many of the proprietors were also on the brink of bankruptcy.

Midland City already had lost one implement dealer, one auto dealer, a hardware store, a tavern, and two service stations. Those who lost their jobs either went on welfare or fought for the few jobs left. Thirty-year-old mothers were waitressing, leaving high school girls out of jobs. Neither of Bill's teenagers could get the jobs high school students would normally fill.

Even the dentist had opened a second office in a nearby town to draw enough paying patients to keep his doors open.

Bill's auto dealership, one of the more successful businesses in town, also felt the crunch. New car sales hit an all-time low, and repairs and parts sales were up. He was still operating at a profit but couldn't afford to lose much more business.

Clearly, Midland City needed a vision of promise, not one of despair. Something had to change, and fast.

CHAPTER 3

The Vision

A month after the Braddock foreclosure Bill attended a meeting in Charles City on economic planning. He found the speaker, Arthur Black, inspiring.

Black talked about community-wide planning and commitment to goals. Those successful in industry, he said, use strategic planning — they establish goals and follow objectives to meet those goals. His message was clear: Communities wanting to thrive had to follow suit.

While all troubled cities basically have the same problems, Black said, thriving ones have the same basic qualities. They have enough jobs for their people, the jobs are insulated from outside forces, and they have benefits that attract families and new industry.

"A wise community sets those qualities as its goals," Black told the attentive audience. "Businesses normally opt for cities that offer tax incentives, have well-educated and dedicated workforces, have reputations for producing quality products, and have good schools and living conditions."

Bill, as well as most of the people at the meeting, was surprised to learn that most of the goals could be achieved without a massive financial investment.

But it couldn't happen overnight, Black said. It would require long hours of hard work and a community-wide commitment.

After the meeting, Bill asked Arthur Black to come to Midland City and speak. Bill was pleased when Black said he would gladly come. Black agreed to July 22, the next city council meeting, a month away.

"You should urge everyone in Midland City to attend the meeting and to participate in the follow-up action," Black advised. "Your success will depend on complete participation."

The next day Bill sent a letter to the city council members. He pondered for nearly an hour before he carefully drafted the letter. He wanted it to be both alarming and convincing.

> To: All council members
> From: Bill Peterson, Mayor
>
> The recent shooting at the Braddock farm should signal to all of us how critical Midland City's problems are. In the past year, we have lost six businesses and 11 farms. Our future is not rosy. It never will be unless we make some major changes.
> I have arranged for Arthur Black, an outstanding consultant on community survival, to speak at our next council meeting on July 22. Mr. Black is convinced change and a bright future is possible for Midland City.
> I will schedule our next council meeting at the high school auditorium and will exempt normal business. All residents will be invited.
> I'm convinced we must confront the future with a plan and not wait for the future to deal with us as it wishes.
> I believe that Arthur Black can help all of us.

Bill finished the letter and then telephoned Terry Brand, editor of the Midland City *Press*. She listened to his glowing account of Arthur Black's presentation.

"Sounds like page one material to me," Terry said. "I'll assign a reporter to write a profile of Arthur Black and his vision for Midland City." The story and an editorial urging everyone to attend the meeting would run two days before Black's presentation.

"I'll assign a reporter to cover Black's speech the night of the meeting. I'll be there, too," Terry added.

"Wonderful," Bill said as he leaned back in his chair and gazed out of his second story window at the empty sidewalks below.

"You know the only way we're going to save our city is to make sure everyone knows how much trouble we're really in, and then let them know how they can help. Since just about everyone in town reads your paper, anything you can print in favor of our cause will surely be appreciated," Bill said as he began to think of other ways to get people involved.

"We don't mind helping as long as there's something newsworthy to report," Terry responded. "And Arthur Black's coming here certainly is."

"I'm glad you agree. Let's keep in touch," Bill said.

"Sounds good," Terry said. "Thanks for the news tip."

Bill called his secretary, Joan, into his office and asked her to start a calling committee to ensure that as many people as possible would attend the meeting.

He telephoned Midland City School Superintendent Helen Sikorski and arranged to have Black's speech videotaped. The district had purchased video equipment two years before primarily for taping high school sports events. Using it for something that would benefit the entire city would be an excellent example of how sharing can take place in a community. Also, using the equipment would show those who had deemed the expense a waste of money that it had been a wise investment.

As Bill continued planning the July 22 program, he decided to request the involvement of State Representative Bill Lund. He personally telephoned Lund and was pleased to hear Lund's acceptance.

Bill was excited to go home that night and tell Samantha, Scott, and Sarah of his progress that day. As he drove down Elm, Market, and finally Mark Street, his own block, he counted 15 "For Sale" signs. Bill was convinced that those people would be sorry they bailed out. If they could only wait a few years, they'd also reap the benefits of living in one of the healthiest communities in the country.

Only the most blissful of words described how Bill felt as he ascended the long driveway leading to his 80-year-old two story brick home. The trim and porch needed a touch of paint and some of the windows needed to be replaced, but overall the house was in good repair.

The lights were on in the kitchen. Sam or Sarah had started dinner, he thought as he brought his Oldsmobile Regency Ninety-Eight to a halt. He wondered if Sam and the kids would be as enthusiastic as he. Scott and Sarah, of course, would be excited as ever. They loved Midland City. They knew its every corner like the back of their hands, from the caves down by the river to the swimming quarries on the other end of town where all the kids hung out. All their friends lived in Midland City — friends they never wanted to leave.

Bill hoped Samantha would be excited too. Hadn't she said that if the city was healthy she would love to stay?

"What's for dinner?" Bill asked as he opened the back door.

"Hi Dad. I've made your favorite — country-fried steak, mashed potatoes, gravy, and fresh green beans from the garden," responded Sarah as she tilted each pan so her father could catch a glimpse of what would soon soothe his hunger pains. Bill had been so wrapped up in his work he had forgotten to take a lunch break.

"Looks scrumptious, Sarah. Where's your mom?"

"Where else but picking up my 'baby brother' from hockey school." Sarah, who had just turned 16 the week before, rolled her eyes in a sign of disgust. "Every time I want the car, mom's got to taxi Scott to this game or that game. You'd think that there was nothing else in this world but hockey. I wanted to go to the library to study for my finals before dinner, but no! When can I get my own car Dad?"

Sarah no more than finished her sentence when Scott walked in. He barely squeezed through the kitchen door with all his equipment. Sweat starting from his matted auburn hair streamed down his perspiration-drenched face.

"What's for dinner, Sis?" he asked.

The stench coming from her younger brother was enough to put her over the edge.

"Nothing, until you take a bath!" she shouted.

"You don't have to yell," Scott responded defensively.

"I'll yell if I want to," Sarah rebutted.

"Stop it, kids. Scott, put your gear away and go clean up. Sarah, you go and help your mother with her bags. I want you all at the dinner table in 15 minutes. I have some good news." Why do teenage siblings always have to fight? Bill asked himself as he poured himself a glass of red wine.

Bill was all smiles during dinner as he told his family of his conversation with Black the night before and of the meeting he was planning.

"Do you really think this Arthur Black can help the city? Haven't things gotten too bad?" asked Samantha, hoping he hadn't detected the sour note in her voice.

"He really believes he can, and so do I," Bill responded.

"Will we still be able to take our trip to Rocky Mountain Park in July?" Samantha asked Bill. "I'm really looking forward to starting my photo essay."

"That's something I forgot to mention," Bill said carefully. He hoped Samantha wouldn't be too upset when he finished breaking the news. "Arthur Black says it's going to take at least one summer of thoughtful planning and at least a year of hard work before we see any apparent changes. I won't be able to take time off this summer. Maybe we can go next summer."

"Does that mean I can sign up for the summer hockey league?" asked Scott excitedly.

"Is that all you can think about?" snapped Sarah.

"Will you kids hush up so your father and I can talk this over," Samantha said as she tried to cool her own temper.

"Can't we try to go in August, or even September?" she asked as she picked at her green beans.

"Well maybe, but for this to work I have to give it my wholehearted effort," Bill said. "Why don't you get involved too, Sam? It's really going to be exciting."

"I'll think about it, but there's not much I can do. My forte is photography, not business."

At least she said she'd think about helping, Bill thought to himself. If he failed to convince Sam of a bright future, who could he convince?

CHAPTER 4

The Town Meeting

More than 2,000 people turned out for the meeting in Midland High School's auditorium. There hadn't been so many adults in the school since the basketball playoffs when the Midland City Cougars went on to win the State Basketball Championship.

All six city council members, Representative Lund, and Arthur Black were seated on the stage with Bill. He expected little participation on their part but wanted them visible and in a position indicating their support.

Bill introduced Arthur Black by listing his credentials. "While Arthur Black grew up in a small town and understands small towns, he has an extensive background in industry and is an expert in processes of change," Bill told the receptive group. "He has helped revive many businesses and can adapt the process to communities like ours."

As Black approached the podium, the audience applauded but seemed a bit reserved. Some were wondering what a guy like Black was doing sticking his nose in "their" town's business.

"First of all, I want to thank you for inviting me to come here tonight," Black said in his opening remarks. "Communities that take action, such as I presume yours is going to do, will rapidly rise above their competition and reestablish their lost economic affluence. Unfortunately, most communities are not like yours, and are wallowing in despair rather than initiating change."

Midland City alone couldn't solve the price squeeze problems on its farmers or local manufacturers, Black cautioned, but it could take measures to improve the local economy through a commitment to quality.

With an overhead projector he displayed a brief prayer:

> *GOD GRANT ME*
> *THE SERENITY*
> *TO ACCEPT THE THINGS*
> *I CANNOT CHANGE*
> *THE COURAGE*
> *TO CHANGE THE THINGS*
> *I CAN*
> *AND THE WISDOM TO KNOW*
> *THE DIFFERENCE*

"Among the things you 'cannot change' are the basics of American business style," he told the audience. "Although you can't make things happen on a national basis, you *can* make Midland City successful compared to its neighboring competition because all American communities face the same federal government handicaps."

Black said Midland City could not change the Wall Street mentality that drives industry to seek short-term goals, farm supports that place farm products at an international disadvantage, the United States' thriftless spending habits, and a general national focus on self rather than community.

He then switched gears and began talking about Japan's business economy with an apology. He said that while he recognized the problems many people have with using examples from Japan, many of Japan's successes are largely the result of U.S. directives.

He told the story of how General Douglas MacArthur had helped Japan become self-sufficient in the late 1940s and early 1950s. In 1946 Japan was a nation reliant on imports for 40 percent of its food, 90 percent of its fuel, and more than 50 percent of its raw material. It had 100 million people, few jobs, and a worldwide reputation for cheap, low quality "Japanese copies."

MacArthur directed the pursuit for quality in Japan's school system. He brought W. Edwards Deming to Japan to teach statistical methods for quality management. Along with Joseph Juran and other consultants, they led the Japanese to work together to solve problems and create products marketable in international trade.

During the 1950s and 1960s Japan sought ways to increase job efficiency and quality. Japanese business leaders used quality circles, statistics, value analysis, and numerous other "American" quality control processes. They spent the money and time to train students and workers, Black said.

"Meanwhile, America sold anything it could produce," Black continued. Its factories were no longer producing bombs and shells; they readily changed from a profitable wartime production base to peacetime products. America focused only on profit-based price increases instead of on improving its schools and industries.

"What Midland City needs to do is to borrow Japan's enthusiasm and dedication to improvement and Dr. Deming's approach to quality control and production," Black said.

Deming, now a professor of Continuing Engineering Education at George Washington University, is world-renowned for his work on quality control in industry. The Japanese government honors him by presenting the Deming Medal to top businesses each year.

Deming's theory is based on his 14 management principles, which range from allocating resources to provide for long-range needs rather than short-term profitability, to clearly defining top management's permanent commitment to quality and productivity. Black displayed Deming's principles on the overhead projector. He and Bill handed out copies to the audience.

FOURTEEN MANAGEMENT PRINCIPLES
by
W. Edwards Deming

1 Create constancy of purpose for improving products and services, allocating resources to provide for long-range needs rather than short-term profitability.

2 Adopt the new philosophy for economic stability by refusing to allow commonly accepted levels of delays, mistakes, defective materials, and defective workmanship.

3 Cease dependence on mass inspection by requiring statistical evidence of built-in quality in both manufacturing and purchasing functions.

4 Reduce the number of suppliers for the same item by eliminating those that do not qualify with statistical evidence of quality: End the practice of awarding business solely on the basis of price.

5 Search continually for problems in the system to constantly improve processes.

6 Institute modern methods of training to make better use of all employees.

7 Focus supervision on helping people do a better job: Ensure that immediate action is taken on reports of defects, maintenance requirements, poor tools, inadequate operating definitions, or other conditions detrimental to quality.

8 Encourage effective, two-way communication and other means to drive out fear throughout the organization and help people work more productively.

9 Break down barriers between departments by encouraging problem solving through teamwork, combining the efforts of people from different areas such as research, design, sales, and production.

10 Eliminate use of numerical goals, posters, and slogans for the work force that ask for new levels of productivity without providing methods.

11 Use statistical methods for continuing improvement of quality and productivity and eliminate work standards that prescribe numerical quotas.

12 Remove all barriers that inhibit the worker's right to pride of workmanship.

13 Institute a vigorous program of education and retraining to keep up with change in materials, methods, product design, and machinery.

14 Clearly define top management's permanent commitment to quality and productivity and its obligation to implement all of these principles.

"With this slide, we have moved into what Midland City can do," Black told the audience. "Any change process that Midland City uses should incorporate these principles.

"Let's look at what management must do," Black said as he displayed another transparency on the overhead projector that listed the inputs, outputs, and manageable items of a factory. He discussed each of the steps management must take for improvement.

Input

Training Investment

Capital Investment
 Buildings
 Machines
 Material

Product Investment
 Design/Development

Output

Provide Customer Satisfaction

Provide Jobs

Provide Return to Stockholders

Management

Leadership
Employee Involvement
Specific Elements

Relentless Improvement of System
Eliminate Causes of Variation
Improve Quality and Productivity
Generate Pride in Company and Products
Capture Greater Market Share
Increase Employment
Increase Profitability

Relentless Improvement of the System

The businesses in Midland City should not sell anything of low quality. They should sell only quality products. Black went on to explain that they need to improve production methods by constantly using statistical measures, team problem solving, and other quality improvement processes.

Eliminate Causes of Variation

Businesses must use statistical data to identify the causes of variation that hinder product quality. Management should lead the company into continuous improvement of product by reducing variation. American farmers are longtime practitioners of this concept. They reduce the variation in yield between plots of land or different dairy cows as much as possible. By reducing variance, the farmer causes each acre of land or each cow to produce the most possible.

Improve Quality and Productivity

Quality and productivity are inseparable. When a company increases quality it automatically increases productivity. Measuring quality compared to productivity is relatively easy and provides a base for relentless improvement.

Generate Pride

"The pride generated in a Japanese company is outstanding and something that Midland City should duplicate," Black said. "A Japanese company establishes its goals so that its employees take pride, and the company reinforces that pride by acknowledging and rewarding its employees for their accomplishments."

Capture Greater Market Share

"Management must lead the company in the proper direction of product development and investment that will capture a greater share of the market, and as a result, build jobs and promotion opportunities. Midland City must capture a larger share of new businesses. It must offer benefits beyond the competition."

Increase Employment

"Japanese companies are always looking for ways to create new jobs. So should Midland City," Black said. "It should always be looking at ways to lure new companies and encourage expansion of existing ones."

Increase Profitability

"Any changes management makes must ultimately increase profitability. This is the bottom line," Black said. "Experience, both here and abroad, proves that these initiatives will result in increased profits."

Black removed the transparency and switched off the overhead projector. He repeated the urgent need for change. "Midland City must establish a plan of action that includes training for everyone, quality measurements to use, a way to involve employees in management, and reward and recognition programs for employees," he said.

On an easel, he listed a number of quality control processes that are widely used in Japan and in some U.S. companies. He explained that they were the processes Midland City would use.

- Statistical process control
- Team problem solving (quality circles)
- Suggestion systems
- Work flow analysis
- Value analysis
- Design of experiments

He noted that the list was far from complete, but it was complete enough to keep everyone busy for a few years.

Bill watched the audience carefully. Black was a bit tutorial but inspiring. At least he had the attention of the best informed, and fortunately, no one seemed to be nodding off.

"We all need to know how to use statistics," Black continued, "but our schools are not adequately preparing us to apply them to all jobs to measure both quality and productivity.

"Midland City needs statistics to set goals, solve problems, and work toward quality in a logical manner," Black stressed.

Black suggested a strategic plan by which Midland City could focus community effort and establish priorities.

"Your goal is to return Midland City to a level of economic affluence equal to or greater than four years ago. Is that right?" he asked. Members of the audience nodded their heads in agreement.

"To do this you must increase the disposable incomes of farmers, increase industry payrolls, increase tourism, and bring in new manufacturing and service industry.

"Your plan must include means that are in your power. And what is in your power is creating quality products and a quality community environment," he said.

"Each person, each organization, and each company must focus on the quality of his or her product, whether that product be a completed homework assignment, a lesson plan, a business letter, the steel a salesman provides a machinist, the parts a machinist provides an assembler, the product an assembler ships to the merchant, or what the merchant sells to the customer.

"Product is exchanged between husbands and wives, clergy and congregations. In short, 'product' is what is between all people who interact.

"Whenever we receive product we want it to be right. We must, in turn, be just as concerned about the product we provide to others," he said.

Black described his vision of a community where the high school students' Standard Achievement Test (SAT) scores were the best in the state, where the industries worked together to build an image where only quality products were produced, and where the restaurants, service stations, and hospitals all cared that they provided fast and error-free service.

"Such a community would become a magnet for new businesses and insurance for success for existing businesses. You can be that community!" he said as he slammed the lectern with his fist for emphasis.

Change, Black stressed, would take work and commitment and at least one year before results could be measured. "Your alternative," he warned, "is to wallow in despair and watch a fine community deteriorate and slowly die."

Black closed the presentation by praising Bill for having enough courage to expose Midland City to scrutiny, planning, and change.

"You owe Mayor Peterson a great deal of thanks. He truly loves your city and is willing to sacrifice to make it one of the best cities in the nation and reestablish its life style."

The Midland City residents applauded mildly. They appeared a little dazed and overwhelmed. Bill rose and announced a 20-minute break with coffee and cookies in the lunchroom. He urged those interested in participating in the planning process to return to the auditorium after the break.

Conversation during the break began slowly. However, it gradually heightened to a productive level. Bill was pleased to hear most people talking about the speech. He hoped that most would choose to participate rather than go home. "Midland City needs a real 'boot in the butt' if it's going to change," Bill commented to his neighbor, Bob Hendrix, during the break.

To Bill's surprise, nearly everyone returned to the auditorium. Most of those who left had gone home to relieve their babysitters.

Bill opened the discussion first to remarks by the council members.

"This is the best idea I've heard in a long time," said council member Sybil Hensley. "I'd like to start planning right away."

"But is everyone going to be willing to share in the work? Everyone already has a job," complained council member Fred Johnson. If anyone was going to be a pessimist about change, Johnson was the person, Bill thought to himself.

"And what about the manufacturers? Will they trust each other enough to be able to work together?" Johnson continued.

"I'm willing to try," said council member Dean Ostman, owner of Midland City Manufacturing.

"We have no choice. We have to do something. If Mayor Peterson thinks this is best, we ought to try it," shouted Police Chief Spetch from the audience. "We need to do something to stop foreclosures and shootings," he added.

"I agree," yelled several people in the audience.

After nearly an hour of discussion, council member Sybil Hensley moved to establish a plan. "I guess I feel the strategic plan Black outlined is as close to our needs as we could get. Bill has bounced it off many of us during the past two weeks and we all seem to agree it could work in our community."

Council member Ostman seconded the motion and it passed unanimously.

"I would like to get things started. We don't have time to waste," Bill said. "However, we can't go down blind alleys either. I suggest we set up commit-tees that include community members to work on the strategic plan, to further define what Midland City's problems are, and to start a training program."

Bill recommended that the city hire consultants, including Arthur Black, to assist in the planning and training.

Bill assigned each council member to lead one of six committees: Angus Taylor would be in charge of increasing spendable farm income; Sybil Hensley would work on increasing industry payroll; Wayne Dietrich would work on increasing tourism; Dean Ostman would bring in new manufacturing industry; Fred Johnson would bring in new service industry; and Susan Anderson would develop a training program.

"I'll lead a seventh group that will include a representative from each of our five local manufacturers. Our objective will be to pursue quality jointly," Bill said.

Bill urged the audience members to sign up for the committee of their preference. Each committee would have one meeting within two weeks and all would participate in a day-long strategic planning session in four weeks. Fred Johnson agreed to share details of the meetings with everyone through the Midland City *Press*.

The meeting lasted until nearly midnight. Bill wondered what Samantha would say about his coming home so late. She had declined his invitation to the town meeting because she said she had too many other things to do. His wife would understand after he told her how successful the meeting had gone, he reassured himself.

CHAPTER 5

The Costs of Nonquality

Bill was surprised to find Samantha waiting up for him. She was in her darkroom drying the photographs she had taken earlier in the evening.

"It's late," she commented as he entered the doorway.

"The meeting was well worth it," Bill responded. "Are you interested in hearing about it?"

"Sure, but I don't want to stay up too much later. I have to get up early tomorrow morning to take Scott to hockey school."

"Speaking of Scott," Bill responded quickly, "we have to have a serious talk with him about his aspirations in life. He doesn't seem to realize that there is more to life than hockey."

"Stop right there, Bill!" Samantha snapped. "Scott's one of the star hockey players on his team. He's worked hard to get where he is. He's only 13."

"That's just it, Sam. He works hard, but only at hockey. He just barely passed the eighth grade with Cs and Ds."

"He's trying, but he has practice almost every day," Samantha said.

"I think we ought to have him cut down on hockey and concentrate more on school. He has to realize that to succeed in life he must excel in many areas and use his talents to their fullest. That's what Black talked about tonight — well not about Scott, but about how everyone in a community must work to his or her potential."

Samantha, anticipating a lecture, folded her arms and dropped into the chair behind her.

Bill briefed Samantha on what he had learned at the town meeting.

"Do you know that most American manufacturers waste about 20 percent of their operating dollars in the form of scrap, salvage, reruns, retyping, and corrected analyses in the office? And 80 percent of those wasted costs are caused by system problems or from errors by engineers, managers, and administrators."

"What does all that have to do with Scott?" Samantha asked.

"Maybe as managers of Scott's development, we've erred by letting him concentrate so much on hockey," Bill said trying to draw a parallel that Samantha at first failed to buy.

"That's ridiculous. Scott's not a factory. He's a young boy who is enjoying what he likes to do," Samantha said defensively.

"That's just it. Just by us not saying anything, we have led him to believe that it's okay not to try to excel at a number of things."

"Our manufacturers have done the same thing," Bill said as he continued to equate Black's talk with his own family's situation. "They've ignored the fact they're cost inefficient and continue on with the status quo."

As Black pointed out, Bill continued, to get people to take the risks that change entails there has to be either a threat or an incentive.

"Nobody wants to stick his neck out if there isn't a reason. Just like Scott. By playing hockey, he gets the immediate reward of praise from his team-mates, friends, and us. Maybe he hasn't worked hard in school because we haven't shown him the rewards or the consequences of doing so.

"What happens if he doesn't get a hockey scholarship? Will he still want to go to college, and will he be willing to help us pay his tuition?" Bill asked.

Samantha began to catch on. "Maybe you'll have to talk with him. I don't think I'm the person to do it. When I was in school all I was interested in was photography and I did okay," she said.

"Even if Scott does get a scholarship, what are the chances he'll make the pros? How would he make a living? Photography is different," Bill pointed out. "We both need to talk to him, Sam. If only one of us does, he'll think that only one of us is picking on him and he'll go running to the other for shelter. What do you say?"

"I'll think about it," said Samantha as she headed for bed. Bill followed her thinking that changing Scott's attitude, as well as most everyone's attitude in Midland City, was going to be quite a challenge.

As Bill lay in bed he almost began to dread the days ahead. Changing Midland City would take a lot of his time and would stretch his limited staff and budget. But there must be a change and Midland City needed his leadership.

Bill knew he had to convince the manufacturers to fully understand and adopt Deming's 14 principles. He also wanted them to measure the "cost of quality" as proposed by Phil Crosby. Measuring all of the costs associated with poor quality would provide the manufacturers with the vision of how much they actually could save.

For the Saturday meeting, he would have them prepare analyses of their own and their top managers' jobs, documenting what they did during an average day and the percentages of time spent on each task and grouping similar activities into 10 categories.

He would ask them to identify for each task what percentage of time they allocated to:

- Normal costs of doing the job.
- Costs associated with preventing errors.
- Costs associated with failure or correcting failure.

It was going to be a lot of work to get the manufacturers 100 percent committed to change. But he and Black could do it, Bill thought as he drifted off to sleep.

CHAPTER 6

The Manufacturers

The manufacturers arrived at 9:00 a.m. on Saturday in the conference room at Bill's dealership. They all seemed enthused. Some already had met earlier for breakfast at Evan's Diner to discuss their presentations.

Arthur Black opened the meeting by asking them to state their attitudes toward change and whether they believed improving the quality of their products was the key to Midland City's success.

Black, pleased with the responses, restated his belief that changing Midland City would involve four steps:

An Imperative

Everyone must recognize a sufficient threat or benefit from change.

A Vision

Everyone must understand the benefits of change. They must know what is in it for themselves or their businesses.

The Process

Everyone must learn how to use the tools, procedures, and processes needed to achieve the results understood in the vision.

The Plan

Everyone must agree on what steps would be used, when the steps would be taken, and who would take them to make the vision a reality.

Midland City already had made progress toward defining and publicizing its vision. During the strategic planning meeting a week later, Midland City residents would define the processes and plans they would use, Black said.

"I want you all to leave this meeting with a full understanding of the need to push for quality work," he said.

Black subdivided the manufacturers into small groups and asked each group to determine what the cost of quality would be for each of their members. It took them nearly an hour to compile the data they had brought with them.

Office and Technical Management	Total Percent of Time	Percent of Time Doing the Job	Percent of Time Preventing Errors	Percent of Time Correcting Failure
Staff meetings	10	5	5	
Customer meetings	5		1	3
Shop problem meetings	15			15
Data analyses	5	5		
Schedule reviews	5		2	3
Bid reviews	10	7	3	
Order signing and reviews	10	7	4	
Training	10	5	5	
Employee counseling	10	10		
Planning	10	5	5	
Community relations	10	10		
Total	**100%**	**54%**	**25%**	**21%**

Dave Barker, director of manufacturing for Midland City Machine, was the first to present that company's data on office and technical management to the entire group. "I have never looked at my operation in this fashion and I was shocked by the waste of labor and materials in every department," he told his group members as he presented his data on a flipchart.

Dave's group members determined that Midland City Machine's "cost of quality" was the sum of the percent of time it spent preventing errors plus the percent of time correcting errors. They found that his employees wasted an average of 46 percent of their time being nonproductive.

Dave anticipated that when he shared this data with his office and technical managers they would be reluctant to admit that their waste ratios were probably higher than the shop's waste ratio.

As the other manufacturers shared their data, they found they all had costs of nonquality above 20 percent.

"You have to shift from correction to prevention and concentrate on finding the real cost for each error, and then eliminate it," Black explained. "There are a number of ways that you can find and correct causes of error."

Black asked the manufacturers to brainstorm for a few minutes and then list what they perceived as their major problems and causes of error. While they represented different styles of business, they had many of the same problems of quality as well as the same causes of error.

"That's not uncommon," Black reassured them. "You are all wasting up to 40 percent of your resources."

The manufacturers had a few remaining comments and questions.

"I wonder just how committed management will be when the process is started," said Harold Leaf, plant supervisor at Midland City Tool and Die.

"I'm worried about our office workers," said Marian Jones, office manager at Midland City Machine. "I doubt that they'll be able to relate to all of this. They'll probably view this as another program doomed for failure."

"We're going to need a finance system to measure the cost of quality," Dean Ostman said.

Black assured them that with proper training and long-term planning, and commitment to those plans, they would reap the benefits of their efforts.

"You need to start to learn the processes for measuring performance and identifying causes of error," Black explained. "I urge you to visit selected companies that have successfully implemented change."

Black adjourned the meeting with his promise to help arrange some plant visits.

CHAPTER 7

The Talk

Sunday morning after church Bill and Samantha asked Scott and Sarah to join them in the family room. Bill had thought long and hard about what he would say. Samantha had too. They were a bit nervous about how Scott would react, but it was something they had to do.

Bill started: "Scott, your mother and I are worried about you. We think you may be spending too much time on hockey and not enough on your grades. We know you are capable of doing much better in school."

"But Dad, my grades weren't that bad last year. I passed didn't I?" Scott became impatient and started to grind his teeth and roll his eyes as he always did when he felt threatened. "Don't you want me to do good in hockey?"

"Yes we do, honey," responded Samantha. "But your father and I feel you are much more capable than that. We want you to go to a good college and —"

"And what? Be a mayor and a car dealer like Dad? Forget it! I want to play hockey with the pros."

"With an attitude like that you'll never make it, Scott," Bill said. He was proud of how supportive his wife had become in the matter, but disappointed in his son's reaction.

"To make it in this world, you have to at least try in everything you do. If you don't, you're going to be known as a quitter," Bill said.

"I'm not a quitter. I've made mistakes in hockey, and I've always come back and scored." Scott had tears in his eyes.

Everyone felt the tension in the room. Scott was confused. He thought his parents were proud of him, but he was starting to wonder. Bill was angry with Scott who he felt was unwilling to try to understand. Sarah was becoming increasingly impatient; she was 10 minutes late for her date.

Samantha was worried a family quarrel was brewing which would evolve into a silent war.

Bill firmly took charge of the family meeting. "We know you're a good hockey player and someday you may be a great one. But if you want to be drafted by the pros, you have to show how well you can play in college. And to get into a college where you will be noticed you need good grades."

"But. . ."

"No buts, Scott, that's a fact," Bill said.

Scott crossed his arms and reclined, slamming his back into the couch. He knew he wasn't going to get in another word.

"Your mother and I have spent a lot of money and energy on your hockey, and we know that it has been a good investment. But we want to spend our money and energy on your education too. You still have plenty of time to bring your grades up," Bill said. "We have decided to hire a tutor to help you catch up. If our community makes the changes we are planning at Midland City High School, you're going to need the help.

"Sarah will help you with your studies, too," Samantha added.

"I don't have the time to help him, Dad. I have my own work to do. When will I be able to see my friends?" Sarah protested.

"Helping Scott won't take that much of your time," Bill reassured his daughter. Sixteen-year-olds sure are selfish with their time, he thought to himself.

"Scott, we want you to keep track of the number of hours you spend on hockey and the number of hours you spend with your tutor and studying," Bill told his son. "Since we agree that hockey is important and something you enjoy, we want you to keep playing. But we want you to spend twice as much time studying as you do playing hockey until we see some improvement in your grades. Once you bring your grades up to a B average, you can spend an equal amount of time on both."

"We want to make this a family affair. We want to help you, but first you have to help yourself," Samantha added.

Scott agreed halfheartedly for the sake of being excused.

Sarah, thankful that she hadn't been the topic of discussion, hurried off to meet her date.

Bill and Samantha looked at each other after their children left the room and shrugged their shoulders.

"Do you think this will really work?" asked Samantha dubiously.

"I don't know, but it's a start in the right direction," Bill responded.

They remained in the family room for the entire afternoon playing Scrabble and watching golf on television. Bill knew he had a lot of work to do for Midland City, but he also needed some quality time with his wife and was glad he took it.

As Bill lay in bed that night, he wondered whether he had been fair in requiring Sarah to help her brother. Maybe he'd buy her a used car for helping Scott. A car would make the task more palatable and fair, he decided.

CHAPTER 8

The Strategic Planning Meeting

A month after Arthur Black's presentation at the city council meeting, more meetings, letters, phone calls, and conversations had taken place than anyone had imagined.

At their August meeting the city council members had tailored Black's strategic plan suggestions to fit the community's overall goal, which was to return Midland City to its level of affluence of four years earlier. They would do that by increasing their farmers' incomes with part-time employment opportunities in industry, by promoting economic growth of local manufacturers, by convincing manufacturers and merchants to provide only quality products and services, by recruiting new manufacturing and service industries, and by training everyone in at least two key processes — team problem solving or quality circles and statistical process control.

To process the mass of ideas flowing about the community, the council members decided to adopt Midland City Machine's suggestion system on a citywide basis. But they faced the perennial problem of money, or rather the lack of it. They needed a substantial amount of money immediately to pay for the trainers, travel, books, and publicity. Changing the city's tax base, which would take months or years to set up, was not the answer.

The council members decided to recommend at the planning meeting that local merchants and manufacturers with payrolls pay a 1 percent gross sales tax. The 1 percent tax would yield more than $20,000 a month, enough to pay for trainers and to cover publicity costs.

They would suggest that the city also assess the businesses 10 percent of their profit from additional sales they gained due to the community-wide effort on quality. The 1 percent gross sales tax would be phased out as the

10 percent contribution on gains met budgets.

Bill had mentioned the idea to some of the merchants and manufacturers before the planning meeting. Many opposed the idea, but when Bill asked for alternative suggestions, they grudgingly admitted they had no others.

Bill opened the strategic planning meeting by asking representatives from each of the six committees to report their findings. Each representative exceeded his or her allocated 30 minutes, but Bill, even though he despised long meetings, allowed them to do so. The enthusiasm was too valuable to intervene. Bill was pleased with how everyone saw the need to work for quality in everything.

"Anything that isn't done correctly must be done again and the costs of redoing are wasted," said Lisa Ryner, owner of Midland Bakery. "Therefore, quality is basic for bakers, secretaries, mechanics, factory workers, and everyone. All of us provide a product. It should be right the first time."

Ryner raised a sign carrying the slogan that her committee, charged with increasing tourism, had designed for Midland City. "Quality Is the Key to Our Future," she read aloud.

The slogan brought applause and whistles of approval.

"It's obvious that Midland City will not be able to reach its goal all at once," Bill said as he regained control of the meeting. "For the first year I suggest we cultivate a citywide suggestion system, start training in team problem solving through quality circles and task teams, and train everyone, at different levels of course, in statistical analysis techniques."

"I'll accept nominations for people to head the suggestion system after the meeting," Bill said. The job would be full-time and would include coordinating publicity.

Bill outlined the council's funding proposal. Some of the merchants were convinced the 1 percent tax would drive customers out of town, but most said the plan was a reasonable way to raise money and would generate loyalty — a sign of working together to help each other.

Council member Susan Anderson then suggested the ideas her committee members had for a training program. They recommended that a core group of Midland City's representatives use the nearby technical institute's training package in *quality circles*. The core group would then train others who were interested.

"Some of our larger area corporations could help mentor this process," she suggested. "One representative should join the International Association of Quality Circles and become the town professional."

Quality circles, Susan explained, are small groups of employees or people who have a common area of interest and expertise, who meet regularly to identify and analyze problems, and recommend and often carry out solutions. The concept is built on the assumption that often the best people to identify and solve problems are those who are directly affected by those problems.

Training in *statistical process control* is available from a number of sources, Susan further explained. "We recommend using either the technical institute or the community college. Both offer the course "Transformation of American

Industry," developed by Jackson Community College in Michigan which was promoted by the auto industry."

Bill then reported what had happened during his meetings with the manufacturers. He outlined their plans to work together on management techniques and still retain proprietary product protection.

"The management of our five local manufacturers have agreed that once Midland City is known for quality products, both business volume and unit profit will improve," he said.

They had established a "Monday Club" and would meet every Monday at noon at Tom's Cafe to share their plans and results.

School Superintendent Helen Sikorski, said that as part of the strategic plan she intended to emphasize academic excellence by establishing new tough rules. She handed out copies of her proposed changes.

- All students will be required to meet established skill levels in reading, writing, and math before they can move up a grade.
- Participation in athletics or other after-school activities will be permitted only for students with a C average or better in all courses.
- Academic achievements will be publicized in the Midland City *Press*.
- Students' SAT scores must be improved.
- Parental support must be gained for all of these changes.

After Helen finished her presentation, Bill handed out a year-long timetable for the several tasks involved in training, changes in school, and the suggestion system.

Bill suggested to Helen that she work with Susan Anderson to search for training in statistical process control and quality circles. Helen agreed that they would have to work quickly to establish the training skills in Midland City schools.

FIRST-YEAR TIMETABLE
DAY-LONG PLANNING COMMITTEE

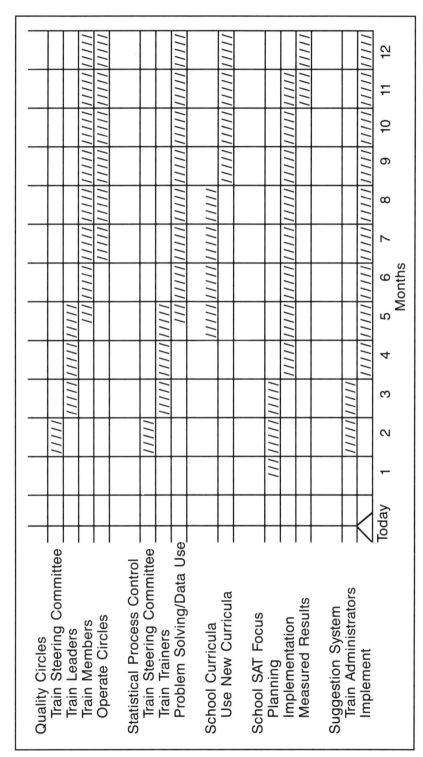

Bill volunteered to experiment with those processes in his auto dealership. He knew he needed to provide an example from the retail area. Arthur Black weeks earlier had told him to take a strong leadership role in the processes. Black said the leadership would provide Bill with both political and technical advantages.

Bill shared the results of his discussions with the manufacturers and businesses regarding the other processes Arthur Black had identified. Bill was pleased to report that each of the processes was set for a trial by one of the businesses.

Midland City Machine would work with *value engineering/value analyses,* commonly referred to as *value analyses.* The company designed and manufactured an extensive line of power woodworking tools. Company President Dave Barker said the process could help improve his product design.

Trock Plastics would work with *design of experiments.* Trock produced a variety of products primarily on injection moldings to customer design. It also had a line of plastic garbage bags sold under a variety of labels. John Trock said the many variables in his manufacturing outfit would benefit from experimental design techniques.

Midland City Fulfillment would use *work flow analysis/work simplification.* The company handled coupon redemption for a number of manufacturers located in the city. It printed refund checks and shipped mail order merchandise. Company President Carol Postman said she was eager to identify the best operating layout to reduce warehouse and office operating costs.

A *cause-and-effect diagram* is essential to determine precisely where wasted costs occur, Bill said. As Arthur Black had suggested, Bill showed the group members how the diagram works by drawing one on an easel as a way to summarize the strategic planning meeting.

"The diagram is also referred to as a fishbone diagram," Bill explained. "It was first used by Kaoru Ishikawa in Japan in the 1940s. It will help us outline the causes of poor quality."

Bill felt confident as he drew the diagram on the flipchart. Black had shown him several times how to do it.

"We have established our ideas and plans based on the standard approach to problem solving. However, by doing this, we may have ignored important points and interactions between those points," he said.

Bill asked the group to take five minutes and think of every cause of poor quality they had experienced, knew of, or could imagine in Midland City. After five minutes, he asked each person to offer one idea and he listed the ideas on a flipchart in random order.

After consolidating those ideas closest in concept, he arranged them according to lack of knowledge and training, inefficient equipment and tools, poor materials and supplies, and bad attitudes. The causes all led up to bad quality.

He wrote "Poor Quality" on the right of the chart and then arranged the causes and their effects according to category.

CAUSE-AND-EFFECT DIAGRAM

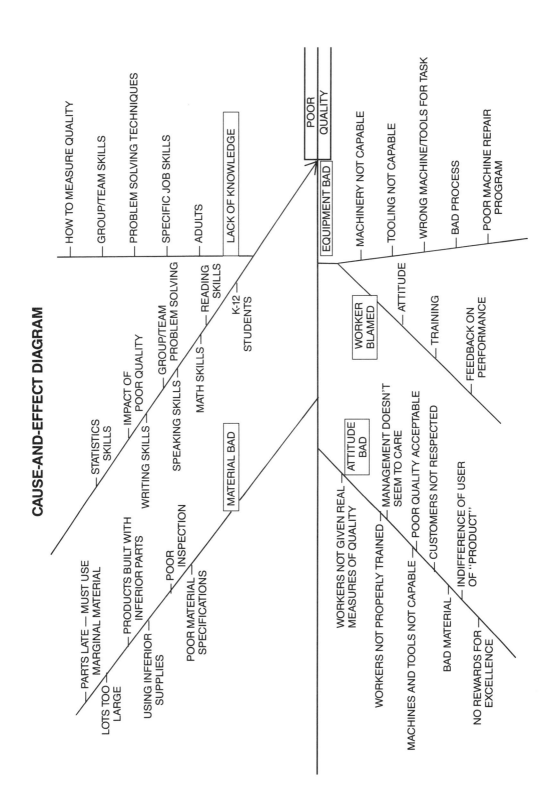

POOR QUALITY

LACK OF KNOWLEDGE

HOW TO MEASURE QUALITY
GROUP/TEAM SKILLS
PROBLEM SOLVING TECHNIQUES
SPECIFIC JOB SKILLS
ADULTS

STATISTICS SKILLS
IMPACT OF POOR QUALITY
WRITING SKILLS

GROUP/TEAM PROBLEM SOLVING
SPEAKING SKILLS
MATH SKILLS
READING SKILLS
K-12
STUDENTS

EQUIPMENT BAD

MACHINERY NOT CAPABLE
TOOLING NOT CAPABLE
WRONG MACHINE/TOOLS FOR TASK
BAD PROCESS
POOR MACHINE REPAIR PROGRAM

WORKER BLAMED

ATTITUDE
TRAINING
FEEDBACK ON PERFORMANCE

MATERIAL BAD

PARTS LATE — MUST USE MARGINAL MATERIAL
LOTS TOO LARGE
PRODUCTS BUILT WITH INFERIOR PARTS
USING INFERIOR SUPPLIES
POOR INSPECTION
POOR MATERIAL SPECIFICATIONS

ATTITUDE BAD

WORKERS NOT GIVEN REAL MEASURES OF QUALITY
MANAGEMENT DOESN'T SEEM TO CARE
WORKERS NOT PROPERLY TRAINED
POOR QUALITY ACCEPTABLE
MACHINES AND TOOLS NOT CAPABLE
CUSTOMERS NOT RESPECTED
BAD MATERIAL
INDIFFERENCE OF USER OF "PRODUCT"
NO REWARDS FOR EXCELLENCE

"We must keep this diagram alive," Bill said as he finished writing. "It represents our level of understanding as of today. I'm sure in the following months we will uncover several other causes to add."

Terry Brand said she would run the diagram in the next issue of the *Press*. Bill said he would have a copy of the diagram enlarged and hung in his office. He added that he would provide amended copies as needed for committee meetings.

The cause-and-effect diagram had done exactly what Black had said it would, Bill thought to himself. It brought into focus relationships between otherwise unconnected actions. It would help each committee plan, and it had enhanced Bill's role as a knowledgeable leader and had reinforced the support he needed to make changes quickly.

As Bill brought the meeting to a close, he asked the manufacturers to prepare monthly summaries on their progress.

"We must share our progress as soon as we can to help everyone learn," he concluded.

CHAPTER 9

The Suggestion System

The announcement of a job managing the suggestion system and publicity for the process resulted in 37 applications. Bill and others from the council interviewed every one of them. The slowdown of Midland City had created a labor pool of very high quality.

They chose Carol Kirk. Her husband was a farmer just outside of town and her children were both out of high school. Carol had computerized the farm records several years earlier and had been working in another town on the local newspaper for three years. She wanted to get closer to home. Carol had completed most of her degree in journalism when she and Joe Kirk married. Carol had been active in the PTA and local politics and knew local people. Bill felt the fit was perfect. Carol had the skills, training, and experience.

Carol started by learning how the suggestion system worked for Pete Ivers at Midland City Machine. It was a challenge to adapt the rules so they would work for a whole community. Carol also found a professional society, the National Association of Suggestion Systems (NASS). She attended its monthly meetings and was given free and excellent ideas. Through NASS, she also found a key book that contained needed guidance on establishing a suggestion system. NASS also identified a software package and prede-signed system called Suggestion Information Manager (SIM), available from Total Quality Systems in Minneapolis. This all added up to a huge amount of information to sort.

It took a few months, but the framework of a system suited for Midland City finally emerged. Carol Kirk worked closely with a consultant to design the suggestion system and to set up the computer software program. The suggestion system included the best ideas from many systems.

The city council members, pleased with Carol Kirk's work, promptly adopted the system with only minor additions and changes.

Carol asked all merchants and manufacturers to reward people who offered profitable suggestions. She suggested they donate 10 to 20 percent of their first year's savings generated by the suggestions to a cash reward program. She also planned four drawings per year for rewards such as color televisions. Only those people with legitimate suggestions qualified for the drawings. Most businesses agreed to exhibit the televisions in their windows on a rotating basis to generate interest.

The Midland City Chamber of Commerce provided suggestion collection boxes and forms with display stands to every business. It also provided the promotion signs that were displayed in their windows and employee lunchrooms.

All suggestions and complaints were reviewed on a citywide basis, allowing City Hall to act as the quality controller. Carol reviewed the suggestions and complaints and directed them to the appropriate merchant, manufacturer, or organization. She monitored follow-up action and reported repeated complaints to Bill and a newly formed business committee.

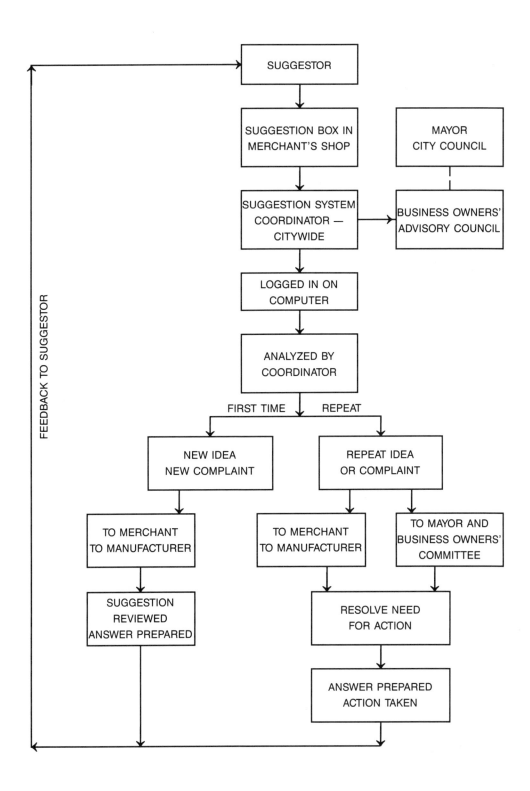

	006160

QUALITY —
THE KEY TO OUR FUTURE
MIDLAND CITY SUGGESTION SYSTEM

Please fill out this form and place in the locked box. The forms will be reviewed by the City Suggestion Administrator and then presented to the proper persons to correct the problem.

THANK YOU FOR HELPING MIDLAND CITY GROW

THE PROBLEM — Please describe the lack of quality or other problem.

It affects _____ Company

THE SOLUTION — Please state how quality could be improved or the problem corrected if you can (use reverse side if needed).

SUBMITTED BY: _____ Phone No. _____

Name

_____

Address

FOR SUGGESTION SYSTEM OFFICE USE
Idea Code _____
Repeat Idea _____
Merchant Notified _____ Suggestor Thanked _____

In consideration of my participation in the Midland City Suggestion System, I agree that the use of this suggestion by Midland City or businesses therein shall not be the basis for a claim of any nature by me, my heirs, executors, or assigns.

As the suggestion system was used, Carol found that most merchants believed that their customers were truly impressed with Midland City's plans. The customers felt they had become a part of the businesses they patronized. The merchants were competing with stores in nearby towns so any advantage they could gain was definitely worthwhile. And they liked gaining something tangible for the 1 percent of sales they were assessed.

The more enthusiastic merchants posted the best suggestions along with the names of the authors in their windows. Some held their own drawings and gave out gift certificates redeemable at their stores.

Of course, there were nonbelievers. Some said they were happy with the way things were and didn't need Carol Kirk or anyone else telling them how to run their businesses. Carol personally visited those merchants to tell them how the other businesses had profited from the system.

Some merchants participated but were hesitant to make the suggested improvements. At the city council's recommendation, the Midland City Merchants Association established a task team to determine how to convince those merchants to improve their services or products. The team included both believers and nonbelievers.

After several meetings the team members concluded that they all could gain financially by participating in the system. They decided that everyone had to participate if Midland City was to have a quality image. But they needed some "teeth" in their enforcement.

After they announced their findings, some nonbelievers remained just that, but about 25 percent of those who originally had rejected the idea agreed they had been foolish in not responding to the suggestion system.

To further enhance participation, only those merchants who supported the system were able to display the televisions and were given banners proclaiming their support. The real pressure came from the Midland City Merchants Association and their families, friends, employees, and customers — or lack of customers as their businesses declined. Midland City residents began to back the system and merchants who didn't became increasingly unpopular.

The pressure on the merchants wasn't organized but it was effective. Local people saw the access to the suggestion system as a potential reward if they found money-saving ideas. There was a shift toward doing business with merchants that were part of the process. A few saw the benefits to Midland City being unified. After only 10 months of operation, Carol found she had nearly all of the merchants participating. Carol gave a lot of credit to Terry Brand for the publicity on winners and the merchants.

As months passed, the benefits of the system became more evident. Reports of dollars saved spurred additional interest, especially from Midland City *Press.*

Carol Kirk was convinced that the suggestion system was the key to quality for Midland City. Besides, it made the process of change fun and profitable for customers, employees, and businesses.

CHAPTER 10

Training

Setting up an adult training program in statistical process control and quality circles was beyond the normal demands of Superintendent Helen Sikorski and her staff. She anticipated morale problems if she tried to force her teachers into the new tasks. But she was determined to find a way.

She hired instructors from the nearby technical institute to train her volunteers who, in turn, would train everyone else. Fortunately, more than enough teachers and recently retired teachers, engineers, and managers from Midland City manufacturers volunteered to be trainers.

They began the two-month training course that fall. Meanwhile, Bill helped Helen form a steering committee of manufacturers, merchants, and school district administrators. The committee's job was to determine the level of training needed at each business and to schedule training sessions.

Helen knew what a massive task it would be to educate all of Midland City's workers. She would have to change her own management style. From what she had read about education in Japan, she was convinced that ultimately, she would have to retrain her classroom teachers to use statistics in their classrooms in the earliest grades possible. But first, her teachers had to learn how to use statistics and accept the need for a curriculum change.

She also knew that teachers were a key element in community acceptance. They were role models and their acceptance was vital.

The steering committee decided what category of workers to train in what order after the trainers finished their courses.

First, teachers and school administrators would finish 20 hours of training in team problem solving and 20 more hours in statistical process control

(SPC) in five months. Math and shop teachers, however, would have 56 hours in statistical process control to allow for more complete training in their subject areas.

Next, managers, supervisors, technicians, and assigned facilitators at all Midland City manufacturing plants would go through 20 hours of team problem solving training and 56 hours of statistics. They would finish three months after the school employees and would establish a joint process coordinating committee so all companies could share what they learned.

Next, factory and office workers at Midland City manufacturing plants would have 20 hours of training in team problem solving and eight hours in SPC. They would complete their training four months after their managers.

Helen had been concerned about training factory workers. Many of them, she thought, would find 56 hours of training threatening. She knew they could learn the material, but some had never gone to college or even graduated from high school because they were uncomfortable in an academic setting. In addition, the team problem solving training emphasized conference leadership, team building, and decision making normally not a part of a factory worker's daily life.

As usual, Arthur Black came to the rescue. He suggested, and Helen agreed, that the factory workers complete the entire team problem solving course, but that their SPC training be stretched over a longer period of time with much of it done through actual working situations.

After the factory and office workers, Midland City merchants, city managers, and supervisors would have 20 hours in team problem solving and 56 hours in SPC. They would finish four months after the factory workers. Then the merchants' employees would go through 20 hours in team problem solving training and 56 hours in SPC. Their training in SPC would also be stretched over a longer period of time. They would finish four months after their bosses completed their training.

The entire cycle would take 20 months. A long, massive training program, but with hundreds of people involved, Helen felt fortunate it would take only that amount of time.

After a month of training, the trainers briefed Helen and her steering committee on what they had learned. They touched briefly on basic SPC techniques, including Pareto charts and cause-and-effect diagrams, and they reviewed Deming's 14 management principles. They stressed the need for using statistical controls during production to ensure that a product is good before it makes it to the inspection stage. They also reviewed how SPC techniques were usable in retail stores, banks, and hospitals. Helen's employees showed how SPC could help teach and administer in the schools.

As the trainers continued their report, one steering committee member suggested that Midland City could easily guarantee quality by carefully inspecting each product before shipment. One trainer, immediately challenging that argument, asked all the committee members if they thought they could inspect a part they knew as well as their employers. Almost everyone answered "yes."

"Do I have a test for you!" the trainer responded as she displayed a test paragraph on the overhead projector, written by Noriniko Nakayama, president of Fiji Tsu American, Inc.

> *You see, Quality Control is not just a little room adjacent to the factory floor, whose occupants make a nuisance of themselves to everyone else. Quality control is, or should be, a state of mind. It permeates the entire operation. Everyone, from president to the production trainee, is part of Quality Control. But it is up to top management to instill in everyone the desire to produce goods of the highest quality.*

She gave them one minute to count the number of times the letter "E" appeared in the paragraph. No one could agree on a number. "Even proof-readers rarely can," the trainer said. She had effectively made her point regarding the difficulty an inspection department has in weeding out a bad product from a given batch.

"The obvious answer is to create a system that is as error-free as possible and reduce the need for inspections," she said.

The SPC course, the trainers said, was organized into a number of sections covering the following material:

- An overview of the international nature of business competition and the resulting conclusion that the United States must either achieve quality production or, in effect, become a second-class nation.
- A review of the impact of Deming on Japan and an understanding of how his principles should be woven into the manufacturing culture.
- The use of improvement teams to analyze problems and determine solutions.
- Effective project selection using brainstorming, prioritization, and analysis.
- How to collect data using flowcharts and cause-and-effect diagrams and how to construct a Pareto chart from the data.
- The measurement of median, central location, shape, and variability of data.
- The development of histograms, distribution curves, and an understanding of the measure of variance.
- The application of data techniques to process control and the use of $\overline{X}$ and R charts and familiarity with other chart formats.
- The analysis of process capability using both arithmetic and chart techniques.
- The use of median and individual charts for process control.
- The use of attribute charts for process control.

Helen was amazed at the depth of the problem-solving techniques involved. She hadn't used statistics since she studied for her doctorate. But for Midland City, the focus would be limited to a relatively simplified process with direct application. With the proper amount of management support, the knowledge of SPC would make a difference in the quality of work.

The trainers had viewed videotapes that explained the "culture" of team problem solving for teams or circles and how people must learn to work as a team and to handle the hostility that often accompanies working in groups.

Team training includes team building, use of nominal group technique, and an understanding of decision-making processes that the team could seek help on if appropriate. Basic SPC skills were to be a part of the team training since the ability to gather data was needed if the solutions to problems were to be found. Nominal group technique (NGT) was presented as a structured form of brainstorming with a voting process to lead the team to a conclusion. The NGT process coupled with seeking data on what was really happening provided the basis for solutions to tough business problems.

Team members are formed around natural work units where they share common knowledge or common concerns. The team members have the knowledge of how things really work and with training and skills can help change the process or procedure involved. The trainers stressed that 80 percent of the problems are caused by the processes and procedures and only 20 percent by employees. With teams, employees feel they have the power to change the system to improve their work quality.

The same trainer suggested that each team adopt a name to give the group members a sense of identity.

"Circles or teams bring about a feeling of old-fashioned team spirit, especially because participation is voluntary. And the solutions they offer through group consensus are far more creative than individual solutions," he said.

Team participants first need to know what is expected of them in order to achieve anything, another trainer advised. Then they must determine how they will measure their productivity. The measures should reflect their output in relation to their input and should be specific, but easy to understand. The measures should be selected by the team, such as number of bad parts produced or number of invoices retyped. The team should collect its own data to measure change. The team needs to be in control of its project.

After teams have successfully solved some problems, they are more able to set reasonable goals for improvement, another trainer said. But they need regular feedback for their members and management on how they are progressing toward their goals.

"Each team or circle must elect a leader and be provided with a facilitator — a person from outside the group who will help guide the problem solving process," added another trainer. "They also need to be supported by a steering committee that includes top managers, to establish policies, objectives, and management support.

"Communication between employees and management is essential for successful teams."

After the meeting, Helen listened to one of Deming's tapes. "It's all so simple — so simple," Deming's recorded voice calmly stated.

The concepts may be simple, Helen thought, but she and the other leaders in the quality program would have to work hard to convince everyone to use them.

It was going to be an interesting process, she said to herself as she switched off the tape recorder.

CHAPTER 11

Midland City Schools

The Midland City school district was a consolidated district that had incorporated the schools from its surrounding smaller communities in the early 1970s. As superintendent, Helen Sikorski had gained immense respect for her work in uniting the schools both physically and spiritually.

Her new task, however, seemed even more complex. She had accepted the challenge of training all interested adults in statistical process control (SPC) and team problem solving or quality circles, and integrating those processes, in one form or another, into Midland City schools. She was determined also to significantly increase the students' SAT scores.

The day after Arthur Black's speech at the council meeting, Helen met with council member Susan Anderson, a high school civics teacher. They reviewed their objectives and formed a steering committee with Joel Larson, the high school librarian, and John Schmidt, the junior high school industrial arts department head.

Their task was extraordinarily difficult. They had to learn new techniques and apply them to a school environment, and become training resources for the entire community.

As teachers, they had learned basic statistics in college, but they had never even heard of the sophisticated processes businesses use to increase productivity and quality. They all agreed that learning and then teaching statistical process control indeed would be a challenge.

Another challenge would be to bring the teachers' union into the change process. Some teachers would resent change and urge their union representatives to lobby for the status quo. Helen knew she would have to recruit creative and aggressive teachers carefully to help plan and implement the training.

They appointed four subcommittees to focus on specific training areas:

1. Adult education in SPC and team problem solving.
2. Elementary and secondary school curriculum changes to include basic statistics and team exercises.
3. The use of team problem solving or quality circles and SPC by school administrators.
4. The improvement of SAT scores.

Adult Education

At the strategic planning meeting, Bill had established an optimistic schedule to train all working adults. He knew that once the adults were trained, changes in elementary and secondary education would happen more naturally.

The classes for the volunteer trainers were held evenings at Midland City High School. The classroom lights burned until 9:00 most evenings as they reviewed the material on team problem solving and SPC. The lights were one indication of action; another indication was the conversation during coffee breaks and at local restaurants. People were using words like "variance" in their casual discussions about sports.

The volunteer trainers were divided into two groups. Although both groups were trained in both subjects, one group concentrated on teams or quality circles and the other on SPC.

When they finished their training, they began training other Midland City adults. Bill, himself, trained extensively in both areas. He was impressed by everybody's enthusiasm.

Town meetings were held twice a month at City Hall with well-known speakers on economic planning, local reports, and panel discussions. The meetings always finished with cookies, cake, or pie, and good conversation. Free child care services were provided in the lounge so all parents could attend.

After a year of training, the adult education committee members began looking at including training in value analysis and work flow analysis, even though they had much work left in teams on quality circles and statistics. They knew they had to keep moving ahead.

Elementary and Secondary School Curriculum Changes

As expected, attempting to change the curriculum in Midland City schools was a hotly debated topic. Some teachers, parents, and students saw change as threatening. Helen Sikorski did her best to assure them that the additional training would not replace previously approved classroom instruction.

Still, some teachers felt they already had too much to do and saw the additional material as a burden. Many wanted to use the same lesson plans and teaching aids they had used for years. Change was risky and a waste of time, they argued.

As a former teacher Helen understood their concerns, but she was convinced that Midland City students were not entering their careers as well positioned for success as they could be.

The curriculum subcommittee was comprised of five teachers, an industry representative, and a professor of business from Meadan University, with Arthur Black as an adviser. They were responsible for recommending how the district could upgrade the curriculum. They met with school officials from a school district in another state that had successfully taught circle techniques and statistics to its students. They met also with industry leaders, who reinforced their belief that students who learned the processes would have an advantage when looking for jobs. Terry Brand carried reports of these meetings in her newspaper.

The committee members found themselves in the role of innovators. Team problem solving, for the most part, was foreign to Midland City schools. Statistics were not a part of the district's traditional training and were rarely used in classroom lectures. Thus, there were few teaching examples available.

A week before school started the following year, the teachers attended a workshop designed to show them how Pareto diagrams — a process for presenting relative order of importance, histograms, and cause-and-effect diagrams — could be used in the classroom.

"A history teacher, for example, could use Pareto charting to show the magnitude of impact world wars or major disease epidemics have on the economy," explained Helen Sikorski during the workshop.

The processes could be used in varying degrees of sophistication at every grade level, she said.

"The objective is to make statistical comparison a basic tool for better understanding in a variety of subject areas. Your students must learn a respect for data and the skills to accumulate the needed data for effective decision making," Helen concluded.

Math teachers were the first group of teachers to adjust their curriculum to include basic statistical techniques. Helen worked gradually to change the minds of the teachers who called the training a waste of time by having those teachers willing to change serve as leaders in the circles and planning teams. Faculty meetings featured how various teachers worked the new methods into their classroom materials. Eventually, recognition for accomplishment coupled with strong persuasion caused most teachers to comply.

Using team problem solving for classroom projects helped to resolve a number of communication problems typical of teenagers, as Helen predicted. The process forced a variety of students to work together — students who normally would not have. Working in teams helped the students build their self-images.

Several students worked in teams to research projects. They used statistics to prepare their reports and to provide logical presentations of facts.

There were problems due to untrained team leaders and participants, but the new teaching methods did enhance student learning. One of the team processes, *nominal group technique,* became a byword for resolving conflicting opinions. NGT became a frequent phrase.

By spring, the students began to expect better quality reports from their classmates and complained when the reports failed to meet their expectations.

Helen noticed that students were beginning to think more logically. The industry representative involved was delighted as he thought of employees having those skills. It was a tough first year, but Helen felt her district would soon be a model for other districts to follow.

The Use of Quality Teams/Circles and Statistics by School Administrators

The subcommittee members in charge of integrating quality circles into the schools found a number of good models to study. Many schools, they determined, successfully use circles in the following ways:

- Administrators and teachers use them to determine school policies.
- Students use them to influence decisions on course content and teacher performance.
- Teachers and board members use them to negotiate salary contracts and policy issues.
- Custodians use them to solve maintenance problems.
- Students and teachers use them to determine discipline policies.

The subcommittee members organized four teams: one with administrators, a second with teachers, a third with custodians, and a fourth with students. The circle members were charged with suggesting how to improve their schools and to attack critical problems.

By the end of the first year, the four teams were operating with mixed success. The student team had suggested several changes — some realistic, some not.

Most of their earlier suggestions were actually complaints about restrictions, water fountains, rest rooms, cafeteria food, and special fees. However, as the team matured it addressed deeper concerns such as how to discipline disruptive students.

The custodian team hadn't really moved beyond complaining about disruptive students, smoking in the rest rooms, and the need for updated equipment. Helen felt the facilitator was not properly guiding that group.

The administration team looked for ways to streamline recordkeeping and audiovisual maintenance efforts. The members created a subteam of office clerical workers who performed a wide range of duties including typing assignments and posting student data for teachers. The workers, who felt they were overloaded with work, fully agreed with Vilfredo Pareto's 80-20 rule: They were convinced that 20 percent of the teachers caused 80 percent of their problems.

The clerical team members listed their most common complaints of teachers: Some teachers constantly requested that they retype material because of last minute changes, many gave them illegible or incomplete drafts, and many turned in their drafts late.

The clerical workers wanted to find a way to minimize the need for retyping drafts, which led to extra work and overtime. They started by

Teacher	Original Typing Pages	Revision Pages of Typing	Number of Pages Submitted Late Requiring Overtime
		THREE MONTHS DATA	
1	6	17	
2	10	5	
3	7	15	7
4	10	2	
5	6	3	
6	3		
7	10		
8	2		
9	10	2	5
10	10	15	
11	3		
12	12	2	12
13	2		
14	4		
15	8	2	
16	17	1	
17	11	18	11
18	2		
19	10	1	
20	10	2	
21	10	6	
22	12	12	
23	10	14	
24	8		

logging all the typing they did daily, noting the times they had to retype drafts and rush orders that demanded overtime. They collected data for three months and determined that of the 93 teachers, only 24 teachers used the typing service during that time. Using a Pareto process they prioritized the 24 teachers according to the number of times they asked for revisions. The chart showed the ratio of page revisions required divided by the pages of new typing submitted.

RATIO OF REVISIONS TO NEW TYPING
REVISIONS/NEW ORIGINAL = RATIO

TEACHER	RATIO
1	2.83
2	.5
3	2.14
4	.2
5	.5
6	0
7	0
8	0
9	.2
10	1.5
11	0
12	.16
13	0
14	0
15	.25
16	.05
17	1.64
18	0
19	0.1
20	.2
21	.6
22	1.0
23	1.4
24	0

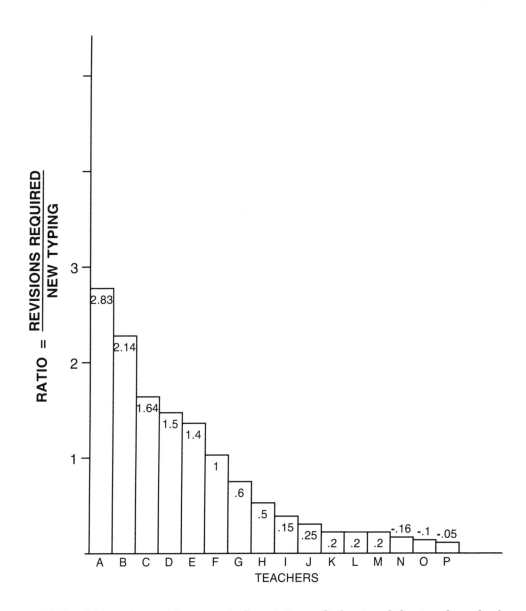

Of the 24 teachers, 16 requested revisions. Only six of the teachers had revision counts equal to new pages they submitted for typing. Helen was faced with a tough problem. The teachers identified as the sources for excessive revisions were some of her best. She didn't want them to become defensive, yet she couldn't ignore the circle's findings.

Helen and the team members arranged a meeting with the 16 teachers. After the team members presented their findings, she added her concerns about the costs of interfering with excellent teachers and asked the teachers and the team members to brainstorm for possible solutions.

Language arts teacher Tammy Lord suggested that the district invest in modern word processing equipment and scrap its obsolete typewriters. Elementary school teacher James Riley recommended that all teachers attend a workshop on effective planning and writing.

"If you're going to discourage corrections, students will end up with error-filled tests and handouts," warned science teacher Bill Simond.

"Whatever we do," Helen assured, "we have to support the staff with positive suggestions and not sabotage it with negative criticism."

Helen divided them into two teams of six. She explained that two teams working independently would bring about the best solutions and also would build togetherness and ownership of the solutions.

After two months, the teams agreed on a recommendation. The district, they decided, should purchase a word processing system with several on-line terminals. Teachers as well as the typists could use the terminals to submit, correct, and update drafts. The school board members agreed to the purchase.

A second survey was taken three months after the new equipment was installed. The total number of corrections and changes had increased by almost double, an indication that more teachers were more frequently revising their materials. Under the old system, some teachers avoided revising their work because the secretaries were always extremely busy. With the new system, the teachers themselves could readily insert corrections. The result was better quality tests and handouts. Bill Simond was pleased that his concern was not neglected.

The clerical workers' labor was down by 15 percent and overtime had been almost eliminated. Teachers spent less time making minor corrections on word processors than they did previously by carefully marking copy.

The faculty team was quite successful in applying the process to salary negotiations. The teachers applied statistical concepts to the packages they proposed and the district representatives proposed. Working as a team they found they could separate emotional issues from economic issues. They were able to present their recommendations to their colleagues logically and statistically.

The Increase of SAT Scores

Helen's call for academic excellence brought her face-to-face with some basic issues:

- The curriculum would have to be strengthened to focus on overall excellence rather than on competence achievement. Students who failed a grade would have to repeat that grade.
- Parents would have to become more involved in and supportive of their children's learning. As a result, their children would have less time for chores and jobs.
- A strict discipline policy would have to be followed to prevent disruptive students from interfering with the learning process.

- And, perhaps the most controversial, the students *would* have to achieve a C average or better to participate in extracurricular activities. Helen hoped she wouldn't have to bench a star quarterback for a bad grade.

Helen knew that she needed to change both the attitudes and practice of teachers, parents, and the entire community. On the surface, such change seemed simple, but in reality, it required a massive change of behaviors.

Designing a discipline policy was tougher than she had expected. Since discipline was a major problem and an extremely emotional issue, Helen decided to use a team of selectively recruited parents, teachers, and principals.

The parents represented the entire gamut, from those who actively supported education to those who didn't. Likewise, the range of teachers included those who rarely had discipline problems to those continually plagued by troublesome students. She also included a junior high and a senior high principal.

Terry Brand gave the discipline team extensive publicity in the *Press*. The more important the circle members were made to feel, the more likely they were to really address the problem, both Helen and Terry rationalized.

At their first meeting, the members agreed that improving SAT scores would enhance the image of their town and would help draw new businesses to Midland City. They believed that disruptive students posed a threat to effective learning because the students often took too much of a teacher's valuable time.

English teacher Dina Harold presented data showing that disruptive students were more likely to come from homes where parents provided little support for their education.

"We need to get after these parents," said Carol Williams, a social studies teacher.

"But troublesome students don't always come from uncaring or unconcerned parents," said science teacher Matt Williams. "Some of these kids are being raised by single parents who don't have enough time to spend with their kids because they're working all the time just to stay ahead,"

The adult group, unable to reach a conclusion, decided that students should tackle the problem. After all, the majority of the students resented troublemakers and showoffs for interfering with their education.

A student team was formed and included both "model" students and those who had discipline problems. The team met with the parent-teacher circle three times to share their views of the problems.

The students traveled to Meadan twice to visit schools with model discipline policies. Each trip was publicized in the school paper and a story was published in the *Press*. After four months they proposed a new set of rules which was approved by 90 percent of the student body. Among other things, the rules prohibited disruptive behavior because it interfered with the desires of the majority. They identified vandalism as unacceptable and punishable by suspension and legal action.

Six months after the SAT committee members first met, they arranged several study sessions for students who planned to take SAT and other standardized tests. They selectively chose samples of test scores from previous years to measure improvement.

The committee members agreed with the teachers that test scores are only one indication of a student's ability. They realized that some students simply are better test takers than others, so they used other measurements too.

The *Press* regularly featured pictures of honor roll and National Honor Society students, and students who were in especially effective study or circle groups. It didn't take long for students to begin competing for the publicity, thus improving their performance. Academic achievement had never before been viewed with such importance.

After one year, Helen was convinced that Midland City was on the right track. SAT scores had yet to improve significantly, but she was confident that they would. She wasn't expecting a quick fix; she was working for change that would last a long time.

A year before, she gladly would have left Midland City for the super-intendency offer she received a week before. But after witnessing Midland City schools' progress, she knew she could not give up what she considered to be the most exciting job in the state.

CHAPTER 12

Scott's Project

Scott barged into the living room where his father was reading the evening paper. He was frustrated.

"Dad, I think you've got me into the final mess of this productivity thing," he said as he threw himself on the couch. "Our teacher has assigned us to teams of five, and each team has to find a new way to use the concepts of statistical process control, quality circles, team problem solving, or overall quality improvement methods.

"On top of that," Scott continued, "she said our grades will be 'significantly impacted' by how well we do on our projects!"

Scott was fuming. His 10th grade social studies teacher said that the projects would teach the students how to do independent research in teams as well as teach them about quality processes. They would have to come up with new ideas, the teacher said, and therefore, they would not be able to use the library and plagiarize someone else's work.

"I won't be able to come up with anything worthwhile," Scott complained.

It didn't take Bill long to realize that Scott was trying to get him to do the homework assignment. Bill knew he had to help Scott, but he also knew that Scott would never learn how to be an independent researcher and creative thinker if "Dad" always did all of his work for him. He discussed the assignment with Scott but specifically tried not to tell Scott what to do.

"You'll have to find a problem with variables that you can measure and use team problem-solving techniques to bring about the best ideas on how to solve the problem," Bill told his son.

The next day after school Scott met with his four teammates at Tom's Cafe. "My father wasn't much help," he reported. His teammates were disappointed. They had hoped that the mayor of Midland City and the leader of its quest for quality would become their source of inspiration and knowledge, and save them a lot of work. Two of the teammates had likewise accosted their parents for quick solutions and had come up with relatively empty bags.

After some discussion they decided to apply some of the nominal group techniques they had learned as the methodology to determine the basis of their project.

As the first step, they each took a piece of paper, and with Scott's leadership, used a technique known in nominal group techniques as *silent generation*. Silent generation calls for each party to spend about 10 minutes listing all solutions that he or she can think of to solve a problem.

After the 10 minutes, they combined their lists of ideas for the project using a round robin method for gathering plus consolidation:

- Improve the performance of the Cougar hockey players.
- Improve the food quality in the cafeteria.
- Improve the quality of auto repairs in the different garages in town.
- Improve the quality of coaches at school.
- Reduce the amount of food waste in the school cafeteria.
- Improve the quality of textbooks in school.

Next, the students discussed each item and rated the measures or data available and the relative importance and contribution each of the quality improvement ideas would have on Midland City. They eventually voted to study how to reduce the food waste in the high school cafeteria.

High school students were served a standard hot lunch, with no variance in the size of the servings. The problem was many of the students, especially the girls, were regularly dieting and threw away much of their food. Also, different students liked different foods. Students who didn't like their food often swapped with other students, but there was still a lot of food thrown away.

Scott and his teammates knew something could be done at the serving line to reduce food waste. But before they determined what, they had to collect data on the number and type of students who ate hot lunches.

During the next two weeks they kept track of the age, sex, and eating habits of each student who ate hot lunch, keeping track of the varying waste day to day and item to item. Measuring garbage, they quickly realized, was a "yucky" job.

At their next meeting they compiled the data and found a definite correlation between students who threw away large amounts of food and students who sought more nourishment every day. Again, they used nominal group techniques to identify potential solutions, to vote on those solutions, to identify the risks of the potential solutions, and to vote on them again.

They decided that food waste could be reduced by offering students five hot lunch options that ranged from half orders to extra portions of everything. To monitor the students' choices, they suggested that a marker system be used. Marker cards would indicate the portion of food a student wanted. Each student would pick up one at the start of the serving line and show the card to the food servers as they moved down the line with their tray. The students would turn in the markers along with their payment to the cashier. The team members also suggested that the payments be adjusted so that students would pay according to what they ordered.

Scott realized he had learned a valuable lesson. By using a sequential application of nominal group technique and touching on decision analysis, he and his teammates were led to an understanding that a simple control of quantity and/or eliminating certain items were not only desirable but almost necessary to reduce food waste.

Soon after the team members finished their report, they presented it to their classmates and teacher. Some students questioned whether the school would even consider such a change because it would call for at least five different prices. Scott and his team members were confident that if public cafeterias could deal with infinite variables, the school cafeteria could deal with five.

After the other six teams presented their reports, the class voted to suggest the cafeteria changes to Helen Sikorski and the cafeteria staff, who eventually agreed to try it for three months.

Fortunately, Scott's team had collected several weeks of data on the exact poundage of waste in the cafeteria. The data provided Sikorski with a base from which she could compare any changes in the level of waste during the three months.

For the first few days, the cafeteria was mass confusion even though the new serving system was heavily advertised in the school newspaper and over the loudspeaker. Students who were not used to making decisions were suddenly forced to determine whether they wanted lunch one, two, three, four, or five. Screaming complaints were heard when students found out they had selected extra mashed potatoes and gravy when they actually wanted half portions.

After the first week, however, the changes began to settle in. The students liked having options, and the food servers heard fewer complaints. Food waste dropped to less than a third of what it had been before the new system. The only party that felt a loss was Torkelson's Hog Farm, which relied on the school cafeteria waste for hog food.

Bill was proud of Scott. He had hoped Scott would find some way to contribute to Midland City's pursuit of quality. The class assignment was an excellent way to have high school students use and understand statistical data gathering and application, he told Scott's classroom teacher.

"I'm thankful also because you gave Scott the chance to earn extra credit," Bill told the teacher. "He definitely needs to improve his grades."

CHAPTER 13

Midland City Fulfillment:
Work Flow Analysis/Work Simplification

Carol Postman was grateful to Pete Ivers at Midland City Machine for helping her start and nurture Midland City Fulfillment.

She had handled Midland City Machine's warranty and customer follow-up services for seven years. But when motherhood interfered, Pete Ivers allowed her to work from her home. She eventually started her own office services business, which in nine years grew to 26 employees and some seasonal part-time help which handled a variety of paperwork and an entire warehouse of products.

Carol Postman had assumed her tightly knit crew comfortably shared ideas at employee meetings. But she found that teams on quality circles and statistical process control enhanced communication among her employees unlike any ordinary employee meeting. She was determined to find out why.

She held a special meeting to ask her employees for their opinions. She was surprised at what many of them had to say.

"When you spent time and money to train us, we believed that you really cared about our ideas," said Linda Fairlane, who worked in the warehouse.

"Before we had the training, we didn't know how to tell a good idea from a bad one. Now we're confident that we won't seem foolish or pushy when we offer our ideas," her secretary said.

Training definitely would be an ongoing process at Midland City Fulfillment, Carol decided.

Carol Postman had become a true believer in suggestion systems too. While she had used the one at Midland City Machine, she really had no opinion about their real benefits at that time. But at Midland City Fulfillment, she actually could see the benefits of the citywide suggestion system, and her employees openly praised the system as a process that ensured that their ideas were carefully considered and responded to.

She wanted to continue her pursuit for quality and productivity by using another problem solving process called *work flow analysis/work simplification,* but she was unsure whether her employees were up to another change. The process was particularly suited to analysis of paperwork flow and product flow — the primary functions of her business.

She first persuaded her key supervisors of the benefits of work flow analysis before she announced her plans to her surprisingly receptive employees.

"The process of change is logical and simple, but it requires dedication and an accepting mind," she told them, drawing on what she had learned from Deming's 14 management principles. "I'm pleased to have such dedicated employees!"

Clem Paxton, Carol's warehouse and merchandise manager, was eager to start the training with her. Through Midland City's adult education committee, they found a number of seminars suitable for their needs and ordered materials from Allan Mogensen of Lake Placid, New York, who had adapted the original process to group problem solving use with involvement of all employees.

Work flow analysis/work simplification calls for solving problems with a five-step approach: define the problem, break down the problem and visualize it in detail, question each detail objectively, develop an improvement proposal, and implement the proposal.

The process calls for the measuring of such factors as the distance walked, or the time that it takes to complete tasks. A systematic questioning of why, what, where, how, when, and who does the job helps to identify where improvements can be made.

After the two weeks of training, Carol Postman and Clem Paxton felt somewhat confident in using the process. Their instructor had used the layouts and data of their merchandise warehouse as examples to explain how the process works. That brought the process into perspective for them and gave them ideas for specific areas to work on.

The two of them spent almost an entire day explaining what they had learned to Jenny Pilon and Helen Sikorski. Jenny, Carol's office and computer systems manager, would use the processes in her departments. Helen Sikorski felt the process could be applied quite successfully in the Midland City schools.

The process, Carol explained, uses a set of symbols that serve as visual aids in understanding work flow. Most problems are solved by a team of trained people that share common sense knowledge in an organized way. Work flow analysis requires learning a process requiring 40 hours of class time that helps understand problems and visualize solutions, Carol stated.

To start the process in the warehouse, Clem Paxton assigned his order fillers and packers to a team to analyze their jobs and determine areas where they could improve. To help determine whether the warehouse layout was as efficient as possible, he provided them with pedometers, a device to measure the distances they walked to complete every task.

Jenny Pilon introduced the improvement process in her departments soon after Clem did in his. She took the advice of several of her teacher friends, who already were using statistics in their classrooms, and started the process by first determining what could be measured and what the measurements meant.

She had her employees list all resources they used to create specific products and services. She supervised keypunch operators, mail openers and verifiers, order reviewers, customer service people, and typists and stenographers. They compiled their lists at an early breakfast meeting.

REVIEW OF WHO DOES WHAT

	Inputs	Outputs

Keypunch	Orders from analysts
	Inventory from warehouse
	Shipments from warehouse
		Order/shipping label
		  sets to warehouse
		Reorders for merchandise
		  to Jenny

Openers	Mail	Verify return addresses,
		  presence of coupons, etc.,
		  to analysts
		Inquiries to customer handlers

Order Analysts	Verified mail from openers	Orders marked ready for
		  keypunch
		Orders with problems to
		  customer handlers

Customer Handlers	Problem orders from analysts
	Customer inquiries
	  on problems
		Letters to customers via word
		  processing and Dictaphone
		  to typists

Typists	Dictaphone from customer
	  handlers
	Signed mail from customer
	  handlers to mail
		Finished letters to customer
		  handlers for signature

"If we all expect to produce quality products, we need a way to define what that quality is," Jenny announced to her staff over coffee and sweet rolls at Tom's Cafe.

"Then our next step is to determine where our errors are occurring," she said to Gloria, her head keypunch operator. "The most critical keypunch output is making sure your people punch in the correct shipping set on orders. I want you to keep track of the percentage of errors you find on shipping sets each week and compare that number as a percent with the total number of orders that come to your department."

Jenny also asked the keypunch operators to measure the accuracy and legibility of orders they received from the order analysts. "Keep track of the ones you have to send back for clarification or rework," she said.

She asked the mail openers to verify that return addresses and coupons accompanied orders. She asked the order analysts to measure in percents the number of incomplete orders they received.

"Diane, I want your typists to keep track of the number of letters you have to redo each week because of mistakes by the customer service people. Keep track of who wrote them too," she said.

Jenny told them that everyone had to keep an account of the number of letters that had to be redone because of typing errors.

In less than a week Jenny began to see fewer errors because of her staff's effort to track them. She realized that some of the improvements were probably short term because they were immediate. She was well aware of the Hawthorne effect, where experiments at a large plant showed that any change in operating practices will sharpen employee awareness and increase quality and productivity for a short time. It would be months before she knew whether the results were long lasting.

As more and more data were gathered, serious problem areas began to surface. Coupon redemption had the highest rate of errors. Jenny carefully read the redemption policies on the merchant coupons and found that they needed clarification. She established new rules for advising clients on how the redemption programs were to be handled.

The customer service department was another problem area. Some employees were having twice as many letters retyped as compared to the average. Pilon had just assumed all her customer service people were equally accurate. She decided to provide a training program to improve accuracy and to let the employees know what her expectations were. She also decided to post the data on errors so each employee had a daily feedback on quality.

All the employees found that the data pinpointed errors in their work methods or equipment errors. For most, the data helped to clarify their roles and responsibilities. The result was a 17 percent reduction in errors in order sets to shipping and improved work quality and productivity.

Meanwhile, Clem's order fillers and packers were progressing toward their own quality improvement goal. They had listed the steps to fill and ship orders and were ready to assemble and analyze their data.

Clem had taken on the role as work flow analysis task team leader and trainer. At the first meeting he explained how to use standard work flow process charting and, with his employees' help, he filled in the data on the time involved and distances walked to complete orders. He sketched the warehouse layout to help visualize what they were trying to determine.

OFFICE AREA

ORDER TABLE

ORDER BOXES

Mdse Racks

Mdse Racks

Conveyor

INCOMING DOCK

SHIPPING DOCK

PACKING TABLE

Conveyor

PACKING BOXES AND MATERIALS

FLOW PROCESS CHART

ANALYSIS WHY?					QUESTION EACH DETAIL
WHAT?	WHERE?	WHEN?	WHO?	HOW?	

NUMBER		PAGE	OF
JOB	ORDER FILLER		

	SUMMARY					■ PERSON		□ MATERIAL

	PRESENT		PROPOSED		DIFFERENCE		
	NO.	TIME	NO.	TIME	NO.	TIME	
○ OPERATIONS	5	.7					CHART BEGINS
⇨ TRANSPORTATIONS	5	1.9					
□ INSPECTIONS	3	.9					CHART ENDS
D DELAYS							
▽ STORAGES							CHARTED BY DATE
DISTANCE TRAVELED	296 FT		FT		FT		

#	DETAILS OF METHOD ■ PRESENT □ PROPOSED	OPERATION	TRANSPORT	INSPECTION	DELAY	STORAGE	DISTANCE IN FEET	QUANTITY	TIME	ELIMINATE	COMBINE	SEQUENCE	PLACE	PERSON	IMPROVE	NOTES
1	Pick up order to be filled	●	⇨	□	D	▽			.1							
2	Move to order boxes	○	➡	□	D	▽	20		.1							
3	Pick up order box	●	⇨	□	D	▽			.1							
4	Inspect order for sequence	○	⇨	■	D	▽			.2							
5	Move to shelf for item 1	○	➡	□	D	▽	60		.4							
6	Place item in order box	●	⇨	□	D	▽			.1							
7	Repeat 4-5-6 2.6 times	●	➡	■	D	▽	156		1.8							
8	Verify order is complete	○	⇨	■	D	▽			.2							
9	Move to conveyor	○	➡	□	D	▽	20		.2							
10	Place box on conveyor	●	⇨	□	D	▽			.1							
11	Return to order pickup	○	➡	□	D	▽	40		.2							
12		○	⇨	□	D	▽										
13		○	⇨	□	D	▽										
14		○	⇨	□	D	▽										
15		○	⇨	□	D	▽										
16		○	⇨	□	D	▽										
17		○	⇨	□	D	▽										
18		○	⇨	□	D	▽										
19		○	⇨	□	D	▽										
20		○	⇨	□	D	▽										
21		○	⇨	□	D	▽										
22		○	⇨	□	D	▽										
23		○	⇨	□	D	▽										
24		○	⇨	□	D	▽										

POSSIBILITIES — CHANGE

FLOW PROCESS CHART

ANALYSIS WHY?					QUESTION EACH DETAIL
WHAT?	WHERE?	WHEN?	WHO?	HOW?	

NUMBER		PAGE OF
JOB PACKER		

SUMMARY							
	PRESENT		PROPOSED		DIFFERENCE		■ PERSON □ MATERIAL
	NO.	TIME	NO.	TIME	NO.	TIME	
○ OPERATIONS	13	2.7					CHART BEGINS
⇨ TRANSPORTATIONS	7	1.1					
□ INSPECTIONS	3	.6					CHART ENDS
D DELAYS							
▽ STORAGES							CHARTED BY DATE
DISTANCE TRAVELED	113 FT		FT		FT		

	DETAILS OF METHOD ■ PRESENT □ PROPOSED	OPERATION	TRANSPORT	INSPECTION	DELAY	STORAGE	DISTANCE IN FEET	QUANTITY	TIME	ELIMINATE	COMBINE	SEQUENCE	PLACE	PERSON	IMPROVE	NOTES
1	Remove tote box from conveyor	●	⇨	□	D	▽			.1							
2	Move to packing table	○	➡	□	D	▽	20		.2							
3	Determine packing box needed	○	⇨	■	D	▽			.3							
4	Walk to box storage racks	○	➡	□	D	▽	20		.2							
5	Select packing box	●	⇨	□	D	▽			.1							
6	Return to packing table	○	➡	□	D	▽	20		.2							
7	Assemble box	●	⇨	□	D	▽			.5							
8	Insert merchandise	●	⇨	□	D	▽			.5							
9	Add packing/padding	●	⇨	□	D	▽	10		.5							
10	1F box is too small	○	⇨	□	D	▽										
11	Repeat 3-9 5% of time	●	➡	■	D	▽	3		.1							
12	F box is too large	○	⇨	□	D	▽										EST COST 30¢ PER OVERSIZE BOX
13	Excess padding & postage	○	⇨	□	D	▽										
14	Seal box	●	⇨	□	D	▽			.2							
15	Affix shipping label	●	⇨	□	D	▽			.1							
16	Move to scale	○	➡	□	D	▽	10		.1							
17	Weigh - add postage	●	⇨	□	D	▽			.2							
18	Place on conveyor to dock	●	⇨	□	D	▽			.1							
19	Stamp shipping copy	●	⇨	□	D	▽			.1							
20	Move to mail box	○	➡	□	D	▽	10		.1							
21	Put copy in box	●	⇨	□	D	▽			.1							
22	Place tote box on skid	●	⇨	□	D	▽			.1							
23	Move to new tote box	○	➡	□	D	▽	20		.2							
24		○	⇨	□	D	▽										

F (bracket grouping rows 10-11)

POSSIBILITIES / CHANGE

He asked his employees to test each task listed on the charts with five questions:

- WHAT are you trying to accomplish?
- WHY do you want to?
- WHERE could this be done better?
- WHEN could this be done more effectively?
- WHO is the best person to perform the task?

The work simplification team members found that many of their traditional roles and responsibilities fell by the wayside as they applied the questions to each task. They gained an insight into how they could use their resources more efficiently according to the warehouse floor plan.

The order fillers found they could eliminate wasted trips having the computer programmed to specify which merchandise to pick up in what order.

The packers found they could avoid unnecessary repacking by knowing beforehand what size box to use. They wasted at least 10 minutes every day repacking products they had tried to pack in undersized boxes and had been wasting shipping and postage costs by packing goods in oversized boxes.

The packers found they could eliminate the reusable order boxes for collecting merchandise by programming their computer to specify the shipping box needed for each order and using shipping boxes to collect the order for placement on the conveyor.

The order fillers reorganized the warehouse merchandise into three groups: high, medium, and low usage. They stocked high demand inventory closest to the order pick-up point, and they moved the conveyer belt from the middle to one side of the room to eliminate the need to run around it to fill orders.

PROPOSED LAYOUT

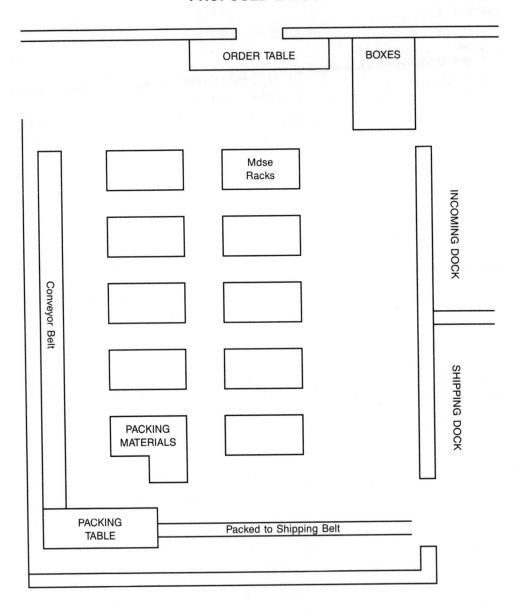

The key was a new software program for keypunch operators to input in Jenny's area. Clem and Jenny found that by working more closely they could help reduce costs and increase the chances of adding new customers.

The new computer software system especially helped new order fillers work with accuracy.

After a few weeks Clem collected the new calculations on time spent and distances walked. He plotted the results on new work flow process charts. He saw significant improvements in order filling and packing. Everyone in the warehouse had reduced the number of steps taken and were discovering ways to increase accuracy. With a more efficient warehouse, Midland City Fulfillment was able to operate without overtime and to bid lower on new jobs.

FLOW PROCESS CHART

ANALYSIS WHY?	QUESTION EACH DETAIL
WHAT? WHERE? WHEN? WHO? HOW?	

NUMBER	PAGE OF
JOB ORDER FILLER	

SUMMARY	PRESENT		PROPOSED		DIFFERENCE		
	NO.	TIME	NO.	TIME	NO.	TIME	
○ OPERATIONS	5	.7	6	1.2	⟨1⟩	⟨.5⟩	■ PERSON □ MATERIAL
⇨ TRANSPORTATIONS	5	1.9	5	1.6	—	.3	CHART BEGINS
□ INSPECTIONS	3	.9	1	.2	2	.7	CHART ENDS
D DELAYS							CHARTED BY DATE
▽ STORAGES							
DISTANCE TRAVELED	296 FT		214 FT		82 FT		

#	DETAILS OF METHOD □ PRESENT ■ PROPOSED	OPERATION	TRANSPORT	INSPECTION	DELAY	STORAGE	DISTANCE IN FEET	QUANTITY	TIME	ELIMINATE	COMBINE	SEQUENCE	PLACE	PERSON	IMPROVE	NOTES
1	Pick up order to be filled	●	⇨	□	D	▽			.1							
2	Move to box storage	○	➡	□	D	▽	10		.1							
3	Remove specified box	●	⇨	□	D	▽			.1							
4	Assemble box	●	⇨	□	D	▽			.5							
5	Move to specified shelf	○	➡	□	D	▽	40		.3							
6	Place item in box	●	⇨	□	D	▽			.1							
7	Repeat 5 & 6 — 2.6 times	●	➡	□	D	▽	104		1							○ .25 ▷ .75
8	Verify order complete	○	⇨	■	D	▽			.2							
9	Move to conveyor	○	➡	□	D	▽	20		.2							
10	Place box on conveyor	●	⇨	□	D	▽			.1							
11	Return to pickup	○	➡	□	D	▽	40		.2							
12		○	⇨	□	D	▽										
13		○	⇨	□	D	▽										
14		○	⇨	□	D	▽										
15		○	⇨	□	D	▽										
16		○	⇨	□	D	▽										
17		○	⇨	□	D	▽										
18		○	⇨	□	D	▽										
19		○	⇨	□	D	▽										
20		○	⇨	□	D	▽										
21		○	⇨	□	D	▽										
22		○	⇨	□	D	▽										
23		○	⇨	□	D	▽										
24		○	⇨	□	D	▽										

POSSIBILITIES / CHANGE

FLOW PROCESS CHART

ANALYSIS WHY?				
WHAT?	WHERE?	WHEN?	WHO?	HOW?

QUESTION
EACH
DETAIL

NUMBER		PAGE OF

JOB
PACKER

■ PERSON   ☐ MATERIAL

SUMMARY	PRESENT		PROPOSED		DIFFERENCE	
	NO.	TIME	NO.	TIME	NO.	TIME
○ OPERATIONS	13	2.7	9	1.4	4	1.3
⇨ TRANSPORTATIONS	7	1.1	4	.4	3	.7
☐ INSPECTIONS	3	.6	1	.2	2	.4
D DELAYS						
▽ STORAGES						
DISTANCE TRAVELED	113 FT		40 FT		73 FT	

CHART BEGINS

CHART ENDS

CHARTED BY   DATE

	DETAILS OF METHOD ☐ PRESENT ■ PROPOSED	OPERATION	TRANSPORT	INSPECTION	DELAY	STORAGE	DISTANCE IN FEET	QUANTITY	TIME	ELIMINATE	COMBINE	SEQUENCE	PLACE	PERSON	IMPROVE	NOTES
1	Remove box from conveyor	●	⇨	☐	D	▽			.1							
2	Move to packing table	○	➡	☐	D	▽	10		.1							
3	Arrange merchandise	●	⇨	☐	D	▽			.4							
4	Add padding as needed	●	⇨	☐	D	▽			.1							
5	Seal box	●	⇨	☐	D	▽			.2							
6	Affix label	●	⇨	☐	D	▽			.1							
7	Move to scale	○	➡	☐	D	▽	10		.1							
8	Weigh - add postage	●	⇨	☐	D	▽			.2							
9	Place on conveyor to dock	●	⇨	☐	D	▽			.1							
10	Stamp shipping copy	●	⇨	☐	D	▽			.1							
11	Move to mail box	○	➡	☐	D	▽	10		.1							
12	Put copy in mail box	●	⇨	☐	D	▽			.1							
13	Return for new box	○	➡	☐	D	▽			.1							
14		○	⇨	☐	D	▽										
15		○	⇨	☐	D	▽										
16		○	⇨	☐	D	▽										
17		○	⇨	☐	D	▽										
18		○	⇨	☐	D	▽										
19		○	⇨	☐	D	▽										
20		○	⇨	☐	D	▽										
21		○	⇨	☐	D	▽										
22		○	⇨	☐	D	▽										
23		○	⇨	☐	D	▽										
24		○	⇨	☐	D	▽										

POSSIBILITIES — CHANGE

Clem saw potential for significant growth. Once he had learned how to effectively plan and measure, working for quality seemed all so simple. He reassured his staff there would be no layoffs, even though he predicted that with increased efficiency he would have a 2.76 employee surplus. He reached that figure by multiplying the number of employees on a job by the level of improvement:

$$4 \text{ order fillers} \times 14\% \text{ improvement} = .56 \text{ person surplus}$$
$$4 \text{ packers} \times 55\% \text{ improvement} = 2.2 \text{ person surplus}$$
$$\text{Total} = 2.76 \text{ person surplus}$$

He assured his employees he would bring in more work to keep them all busy. After all, without their cooperation and work flow analysis-work simplification, he would have overtime costs and would have to bid much higher on new jobs.

Carol was ecstatic about the substantial savings available in what she had thought was already a modern, well-run, and highly competitive organization. She wasn't about to let anyone go.

Helen watched carefully as the changes were made. Warehouse experience seemed to relate to custodial operations at the school. The office and computer activities related to the school administration operations. Helen could see real benefits in the process in a wide variety of organizations.

CHAPTER 14

Midland City Machine: Value Analysis

Pete Ivers had been president of Midland City Machine for eight years, during which time his business nearly doubled. He was the largest employer in Midland City with 140 employees on his payroll.

Due to the size of his organization, Pete and his top executives routinely attended business leadership conferences and were well aware of the importance of effective management.

Midland City Machine produced a line of woodworking tools and machines for industrial cabinet shops and "wealthier" home craftsmen. His products had become standard in schools and cabinet shops. But in recent months his product costs were increasing, and he was losing ground to competitors who could offer their products at lower prices, particularly those who had plants in third world countries where labor costs were a fraction of his.

Pete had to find a way to both increase sales and reduce costs, and he had to do so fairly soon.

He had his employees train for 56 hours in statistical process control and quality circles during a two-year period. The classes were held in the evening, and Pete paid a standard hourly rate for the time spent in class to everyone who successfully completed the courses.

Overall, his employees welcomed the training, but some viewed the teams of circles as threatening. His machine area foreman felt teams would reduce his authority and provide his people with a way to avoid his directives; some of his engineers found using statistical process control troublesome. Having to set up charts for each machine, they thought, increased their workload unnecessarily and they grew defensive as the resulting data began to uncover engineering and management as the source of 80 percent of the errors. They did not want to admit that they were among those contributing the most errors.

Pete spent a fair amount of time reassuring his employees that the processes benefited everyone. Only seven employees were so negative that they were excused from the training.

Three months before they completed their training, Pete noticed that team participants had begun to take their roles more seriously than they had in the past. Early suggestions tended to focus on pet gripes, such as parking lot assignments, cafeteria food, and dirty rest rooms. But as the teams matured and learned to use statistical process control, and the nominal group technique the focus switched to product and process problems.

Pete was surprised that the teams' data paralleled Deming's predictions for all manufacturers. Nearly 80 percent of his company's errors were traceable to his professional staff and only 20 percent were tied to machine operators and assembly workers.

The marketing and sales team used statistics to study costs and selling prices on all products. They uncovered several problem areas, most of which were traced to older product designs, especially the design of the wood lathe.

Pete suggested they use a method for design evaluation called *value analysis* to uncover ways to improve the design. Midland City Machine had been selling the same lathe for more than 30 years. He hired Roger Syverson, a value analysis consultant to train him, his manufacturing foreman, two of his engineers, his sales manager, his quality manager, and his traffic manager. Once trained themselves, they would train the rest of his employees with the consultant's help.

Pete invited John Trock of Trock Plastics to train in value analysis because Trock Plastics supplied Midland City Machine's molded parts. Superintendent Sikorski asked to have one of her teacher/trainers participate too. The entire training team represented thinking on product design, customer needs, manufacturing, quality, shipping, subcontract, and future training. A good combination, Pete reassured them.

The training took two weeks of half days. At the first session, Roger Syverson reviewed the history of value analysis. He said that value analysis, along with statistical process control and work simplification, was rarely used by Americans after World War II. American manufacturers had 20 years of market demand for everything they could produce so they generally ignored efficiency and quality measures. At the same time, however, Japanese study teams were eager disciples of the processes and had found effective ways to use them, he said.

"In recent years," he said, "the Society of Japanese Value Engineers has grown by leaps and bounds while American use of the processes has held steady — another indication of American complacency."

Syverson explained that "value analysis" has been used in medical offices and service organizations as well as manufacturing plants. A brainchild of Lawrence Miles of General Electric Company, it was developed in 1947 to define the organized step-by-step process and techniques used to minimize costs in the design, development, production, and maintenance of systems or services.

"Thus, it purposefully forces a search for the best value in office procedures too," the consultant said. "It is not just a manufactured product design enhancement process, although it is particularly effective in that area."

The consultant used a number of case studies that he said would provide examples of the kinds of problems value analysis had solved effectively. One problem had to do with a purchasing department that had reduced paperwork and the time used to place orders. Another application involved encouraging vendors to generate cost savings ideas. A third problem had to do with an insurance company wanting to increase the efficiency of its claims processing.

After examining the studies, the team members were convinced they were learning a valuable and versatile tool.

Pete Ivers and John Trock noticed how value analysis, work simplification, and other problem-solving processes seemed to overlap. They were unsure of which one would best meet their needs. As usual, Arthur Black had an answer. They met with Black for lunch on a Friday.

As in almost any situation, Black explained, there are several steps in solving a problem. "You have to determine how big the problem is, where it is coming from, and any other details isolating the cause," he said. "Statistics, cause-and-effect diagrams, Pareto analysis, and process control charts are tools you can use to identify problems."

Correction involves analysis using a variety of tools depending on the situation, he explained. Value analysis, work simplification, design of experiments, and Kepner-Tregoe are common tools used for analysis.

"The processes must gain from the best ideas of all involved," he continued. "Most stress team problem solving by employee teams or quality circles. A suggestion system provides a method for rewarding individuals or teams and to provide a process for employees who tend to work alone to share their ideas.

Pete Ivers realized that he, indeed, was headed down the right path.

The consultant tailored his lectures on value analysis to focus on the redesign of Midland City Machine's lathe. Each part of the lathe, he said, had to be scrutinized by asking six questions:

1. What is the item?
2. What does it do?
3. What must it do?
4. What does it cost?
5. What else could do the job?
6. What does that cost?

Then he asked the team to review the lathe project against eight criteria to weed out steps that would not be effective use of its time:

1. Does the product need profit or cost improvement?
2. Will the product have a future of two or more years of active life?

3. Are sales forecasts and production schedules known?
4. Are documentation and cost data available?
5. Does annual sales volume warrant study expenditures?
6. Will technical expertise be available?
7. Will teams get management assistance?
8. Are hardware, prints, documentation, concepts, and work flow diagrams available?

The lathe had been designed in the late 1950s and was a slightly scaled down version of the heavy commercial machines used in industry. About 4,000 of them were sold each year at a total of $1.2 million or 8 percent of the company's sales. The team determined that the current design of the lathe would be in demand for at least the next two years, but competitors were heavily moving into the market. Midland City Machine seriously needed a new, more effective lathe design to compete.

The team members had gained the analytical tools in value analysis and had access to hardware samples and a wealth of consumer preference surveys as well as information about their competitors' products, including customer problem reports and several models of the competitors' lathes to dissect and compare. Their scope of analysis would have to be as broad as possible, the consultant said.

Using a chart, the consultant reviewed the five steps of value analysis: the information phase, the speculative phase, the planning phase, the execution phase, and the reporting phase.

JOB PLAN SCHEDULE
SET SPECIFIC PHASE DATE

MON.	TUE.	WED.	THUR.	FRI.	MON.	TUE.	WED.	THUR.	FRI.

INFORMATION PHASE

QUESTIONS
1. WHAT IS IT?
2. WHAT FUNCTIONS MUST IT PERFORM?
3. WHAT FUNCTIONS DOES IT PERFORM?
4. WHAT DOES EACH FUNCTION COST?

TECHNIQUES
- DEFINE THE FUNCTIONS
- DETERMINE BASIC AND SECONDARY FUNCTION
- ASSIGN FUNCTION WORTH
- ALLOCATE COST TO FUNCTIONS

SPECULATIVE PHASE

QUESTIONS
5. WHAT ELSE WILL PERFORM EACH FUNCTION?

TECHNIQUES
- BLAST — THEN REFINE
- FORMAL BRAINSTORM
- OVER SIMPLIFY
- ELIMINATE FUNCTIONS

PLANNING PHASE

- SIFT RESULTS OF BRAINSTORM
- PUT $ ON EVERY IDEA
- ESTABLISH ALTERNATE PLANS
- ASSIGN WORK AND SET DATE FOR RESULTS

EXECUTION PHASE

QUESTIONS
5. WHAT ELSE WILL PERFORM EACH FUNCTION?
6. WHAT DOES EACH FUNCTION NOW COST?

TECHNIQUES
- REFINE RESULTS
- EVALUATE BY COMPARISON
- COST NEW WAYS TO ACHIEVE FUNCTIONS
- USE STANDARDS

REPORTING PHASE

TECHNIQUES
- SHOW COMPARISON COST (BEFORE-AFTER)
- BE BRIEF
- BE SPECIFIC
- SPECIFY ACTION RECOMMENDED
- FIND AND REMOVE ROAD BLOCKS

"The cardinal rules of information gathering are recording everything and challenging everything," the consultant said.

The team diagnosed the lathe parts and scrutinized the competitors' models. The consultant then explained the functional analysis system technique (FAST), which calls for a detailed analysis of the costs and purposes of each part. They used a Pareto chart to analyze costs and usage of the parts and statistics to help focus on areas where they could find the greatest value improvement.

The challenge of the speculative phase was to collect all their ideas for solutions and improvements. The consultant suggested that the team use the nominal group technique, a form of brainstorming that strongly encourages total participation.

The consultant walked the group members through a creative thinking exercise to loosen their minds in much the same way athletes loosen their bodies before competing. The process was simple. The consultant held up a box of baking soda and asked the members to list all of its uses. Their answers included dozens of uses including cooking, teeth cleaning, scouring, cleaning car batteries, and absorbing odors in refrigerators.

"How many of those uses do you think were part of the original baking soda marketing plan?" the consultant asked. "Would the product manufacturer have packaged and marketed the product differently if he had had those uses in mind?"

The team members, applying the exercise to the lathe, identified a variety of additions and changes, including varying the length of the lathe's bed to meet customers' needs, reducing the weight of the lathe to save costs in shipping and handling, and adding a work light.

In the evaluation phase, the team members determined the feasibility of each idea according to potential benefits and risks. They prioritized their ideas according to whether they would increase customer satisfaction, sales, and or profits. They then determined if each idea was usable, unusable, or had possible future use.

During the development phase, they reviewed the costs and savings that each of the selected plans would bring. Realizing that much of their reasoning was moving toward increasing customer satisfaction, they asked their marketing manager to join their team and arranged to have field representatives offer ideas and criticism.

After three months of applying value analysis the team members proposed a new lathe design. With the new design, they figured Midland City Machine could reduce the selling price of each lathe from $300 to $220, increase profit by $30 per unit, increase profit percentage of sales by 13 percent, and reduce the shipping cost per unit by $10.80.

RECOMMENDED NEW LATHE

General Features

1. Maintains the same capabilities for doing quality work.
2. Reduces shipping weight by 40 percent.
3. Allows lathe ways to be sold in varying lengths to suit customer need/work space.
4. Allows headstock to be configured for large bowl turning.
5. Allows easy belt replacement.
6. Promotes add-on sales.

   - Special stand
   - Variable speed motor/drive
   - Duplicator attachment
   - Tool rests
   - Turning tools
   - Work light
   - Special tail stock for through boring

Design Details

Headstock
Welded members with machining only on final bore for spindle bearings and mounting screw holes. Single end spindle. Ways mount into holes in headstock for rapid removal. Mounting point for work light included.

Ways
Tubular steel ways supported by headstock and stamped saddle bracket at tail. Can be cut to any length. Easily removed from headstock.

At $220 per lathe, they calculated, the company could sell 4,000 more units a year for a total sales volume of $1.7 million and profit of $240,000. Total sales for add-on parts, such as motors and stands, would total $820,000 for a profit of $82,000.

The company would gain a total of $2.5 million more in sales and $174,000 more in profits.

The team members became believers in value analysis. They had come up with major recommendations that would increase sales, profit, and customer satisfaction.

Pete Ivers was confident that his team had done its job carefully and anticipated few problems when he would turn the proposal over to the rest of his engineering and production teams for review and implementation. He celebrated by inviting everyone on the team to lunch to toast a job well done.

CHAPTER 15

Midland City Motors

Bill Peterson considered himself a good businessman as well as a good mayor. Since he had taken over Midland City Motors for his father 16 years earlier, his workforce had more than doubled to 30 employees.

He sold many cars to people in Meadan, the capital city 70 miles away. His overhead, taxes, and labor costs were low. His sales ranked fourth in the state for Oldsmobile dealerships and he could get the same volume rebates as the best dealers in Meadan.

But the local economic downturn began to take its toll on Midland City Motors too. New car sales hit an all-time low and repairs and used car sales went up. Fortunately, Bill had built a good repair and used car sales business based on fair prices, friendly service, and quality work.

He kept his repair shop open evenings and Saturdays and provided loaner cars to customers so they could go on with their business or pleasure while their cars were being fixed.

Bill wondered if his employees truly needed training in statistical process control and quality circles. He employed 12 mechanics, one foreman, two people in the parts department, eight sales people, one sales manager, two clerical workers, one accountant, two janitors, and one driver to pick up parts. They had already developed a reputation for quality work and service.

How much could the processes help an already good operation? he wondered.

A lot, he found out.

Midland City's service industries started training 10 months after the strategic planning meeting. Bill's employees completed their training five months after that.

Bill assigned his sales, maintenance, and office employees to one team, which he called the office team, and his mechanics and parts people to another, which he named the shop team. The office team met every Tuesday morning for breakfast at Tom's Cafe. The shop team met at the same time and place on Thursday mornings.

Bill was surprised at what emerged after only a few meetings: His company's "small town culture" that seemed so open to communication was reluctant to point out the deficiencies of their "neighbors." His employees definitely needed to learn how to talk about problems without being paranoid.

At Arthur Black's advice, Bill attended every other meeting of both groups, rather than all of the meetings. That way his employees could comfortably disagree with his policies in his absence, and gain his support on issues at the meetings he attended.

The office circle was charged with choosing the best merchandising methods for both new and used cars. Bill's sales representatives continually complained about insufficient showroom space and how cars were selected for the showroom.

"There's got to be a better way of selecting which cars go in the showroom than just allowing the sales manager to make that decision," said Julie Danielson, Midland City Motors accountant, at one of the office team's earlier meetings.

"Couldn't we use statistics to help influence sales and to help the sales reps close a sale on the first visit?" she asked.

The office employees skimmed through their data on how many of each car model and body type were sold each month nationwide, regionally, and at Midland City Motors. They tried to correlate that data with the cars that were displayed.

"One problem is that we do not change the showroom models on the first of the month," sales manager Lisa Raymond pointed out. "As a result, we cannot use the sales data to show how showroom display impacts monthly sales."

"I recommend that from now on we change showroom models to coincide with the sales data and study whatever impact that has on sales," she suggested.

Bill and the circle members agreed.

After six months, they compared sales of models that were not on the showroom floor to the sales of models that were. They calculated the sales impact by subtracting sales of models not on the showroom floor from those that were and plotted the results on a Pareto chart.

SALES IMPACT

Model	National Ranking Sales by Model	Average Sales Impact		January	February	March	April	May	June
A (2D) Std	(1)	69.5-54	= 15.5	x68	51	52	56	x71	57
(4D) Std	(7)	20.6-12	= 8.6	10	x18	17	x21	9	x23
(2D) Del	(2)	22.0-17.6	= 4.4	25	x22	20	14	14	15
(4D) Del	(8)	19.0-12.75	= 6.25	7	12	x18	16	x20	16
				110	103	107	107	114	111
B (2D) Std	(3)	23.5-16	= 7.5	x21	16	15	17	16	x26
(4D) Std	(10)	21.0-13	= 8	16	x21	14	16	10	9
(2D) Del	(4)	22.5-18.5	= 4	19	12	x22	x23	21	22
(4D) Del	(14)	10.0-8.4	= 1.6	x10	9	8	7	10	8
(2D) Spt	(6)	27.0-17	= 10	14	x23	x28	20	x30	x27
				80	81	87	83	87	92
C (2D) Std	(9)	16.3-10.3	= 6	9	8	x16	x17	14	x16
(4D) Std	(13)	9.0-8.2	= 0.8	6	10	8	8	x9	9
(2D) Del	(11)	18.0-10	= 8	8	10	12	10	x18	10
(4D) Del	(5)	26.0-18.6	= 7.4	x26	21	16	x24	19	x28
(2D) Convt	(12)	1.4-1	= .4	x1	x2	x2	x2	1	0
				50	51	54	61	61	63

X = On floor that month

Calculation for average sales impact:

Minus
Average sales with display model
Average sales without display model

_____

Difference = Coverage unit sales improved average sales impact

UNIT SALES IMPACT FROM MODEL DISPLAY

```
        0             5            10                 15
        ┌──────────────────────────────────────────────────
C       │ 2 Door Std │ A /////////////////////////////// /
a       │ 4 Door Std │ A ///////////// //
r       │ 4 Door Std │ B ////////
        │ 2 Door Std │ C /////
T       │ 4 Door Del │ A ///
y       │ 4 Door Std │ B ///
p       │ 2 Door Std │ B //
e       │ 4 Door Del │ C //
        │ ////////////// //        2 Door Std C
        │ /////////                2 Door Del B
        │ //////////               2 Door Del A
        │ //////                   4 Door Del B
        │ ////                     4 Door Std C
        │ //                       2 Door Convert C
```

They were proud of the way they had used statistics. Some of the circle members thought they'd never understand how to use them or ever find a way to use them in car sales. Also, working as a team made them less at odds with each other. Working together on a problem gave them a new respect for each other.

Bill was amazed at the impact the showroom had on sales, even though he was well aware that impulse buying is a major force in car sales. He knew his business was heavily impacted by showroom display because he had many out of town buyers who bought their cars during their first visit. From the office circle's findings he learned which models to show to maximize impulse buying.

The office circle members continued to explore ways to optimize showroom use. They wanted to present a "plush image" to their customers, but most of them came to Midland City for a bargain. If they found a bargain plus royal treatment, they'd surely come back to and tell their friends about Midland City Motors.

"We need to promote our services more," said sales representative Joe Biden during one meeting. "We could start by advertising our free loaner car service."

"And on rainy days, we could have valet parking for customers," said
secretary Jill Jordan. "The customers could drive into the garage and the
runners could park their cars so they wouldn't have to get out in the rain
to shop for a new car."

Custodian Jerry Herman suggested they offer tours of the service area.

"Of course we would have to keep the area super clean, but the real
benefits of the tours would be increased sales. Customers are influenced by
a sparkling clean shop, you know," Herman said.

Joe Biden had one of the best ideas. He suggested that they use a new
dealer emblem in chromed cast metal that would read "Quality Service by
Midland City Motors." The emblem was right in line with Bill's beliefs in
his company. He ended up ordering new emblems not just for new cars, but
as replacements for the old emblems on used cars they resold.

Bill saw benefits in all the ideas. His repair shop was clean, but it was
hardly a showplace. Besides, the insurance company discouraged allowing
customers in work areas. But he agreed to suggest the tour idea to the shop
team and arrange a joint circle meeting to address the idea.

The shop team's goal was to generate better quality and more efficient
work in the shop while reducing costs. To review quality, four of the team
members kept track of how fast and accurate shop work was done and the
number of parts that failed before and after they had been installed. They
documented each shop order that had to be reordered from the manufacturer
and each part that had to be reinstalled.

They found that only 12 percent of all of the work done in the shop was
rework, and 5 percent of the rework could be attributed to mechanic error.
The rest of the rework was due to bad parts. The manufacturers of replacement parts that caused 46 percent of the problems only sold Midland City
Motors 17 percent of its parts. Those suppliers had caused more than twice
their share of errors and costly rework. Bill contacted the appropriate
suppliers to resolve the quality problems. He brought his business to other
suppliers when problems couldn't be resolved.

The shop team found that shop employees spent too many hours waiting
in line for parts.

"Mechanics can't be waiting in line at the parts window, while the parts
department hunts down parts and completes paperwork," said head mechanic Dan Riskon, at one of the meetings.

The team members discussed that problem at great length and toured
several shops in Meadan for solutions. They had learned from their statistics
training that statistics had to be gathered with a vision of the probable result.
With no data base to use in a statistical analysis of the problem, they had
to find a way to envision the possible result and collect new data to be as
efficient as possible.

First, they needed to know how each mechanic spent his or her day. They
selected a process, offered by a consultant in Meadan, which involved taking
a random time sampling. They gave a daily log form to each mechanic. At
random intervals each day a klaxon was sounded to signal that it was time

for each mechanic to write an "X" and the time next to the description of the task on which he or she had been working. The consultant used a computer to analyze the data and reported the results to the mechanics weekly.

MIDLAND MOTORS MECHANICS

WORK BEING DONE IDENTIFICATION CARD

NAME _____ DATE _____

Working on repair							
Diagnosing problem							
Consulting on problem							
Assisting on repair							
Talking to foreman							
Talking to parts department							
Making up parts list							
Waiting for parts							
Completing parts paperwork							
Completing work order							
Road testing							
Cleaning up bay							
On break							
Other							

After a month, it became clear that waiting at the parts department was taking up 11.6 percent of the mechanics' time.

At the recommendation of the shop team, Bill provided four mechanics and the parts department with two-way radios. The mechanics used the radios to order parts as they worked on or under cars. Thus, the parts department could have the parts ready when the mechanics came to the window.

The following month, the mechanics again logged their work as the klaxon sounded. The results were significant. The four mechanics who used the radios spent only 2 percent of their time at the parts desk picking up parts.

That was a savings of 9.6 percent per mechanic, or a 38.4 percent savings for all four.

Sometimes a mechanic wanted parts that hadn't arrived from the factory, hadn't been unpacked, or were at another dealership. The radios provided early notification to the people who worked the parts desk, allowing them to begin searching for parts before the last minute.

The outstanding results were enough to convince Bill to buy radios for all of his mechanics. Some of the mechanics who originally had shunned the idea were quickly convinced otherwise. After all, they had an incentive program and were rewarded for jobs completed. They soon realized that the radios were just another tool for them to make money.

Bill had his office team members use the same random time sampling process in their departments. Their results were also significant.

Bill was eager to share his results with everyone in Midland City. He decided to share them with Bill Saxon of Saxon Motors — maybe not all the details on the showroom setup, but at least enough to tempt Saxon to design an emblem like "Saxon Motors, featuring Midland City Quality."

Midland City would not flourish with merchants battling over existing business, he rationalized. Midland City's future depended on its ability to bring in new business and to be recognized as having the best business climate in the state.

CHAPTER 16

Local Merchants

It was more than a year after the strategic planning meeting and the citywide suggestion system was in full swing. Midland City residents were becoming increasingly aware of their right to quality. They disliked cold coffee, stale donuts, and shoddy clothing, and were no longer willing to pay for substandard products.

Many Midland City merchants originally felt they had no need for statistical process control and quality circles or teams. Most of them employed four to 15 people and believed that their employees already talked to each other on a regular basis.

After considering the numerous comments they had received, the merchants knew, whether they admitted it or not, that they had to improve their products and services. Bill Peterson stood behind the training 100 percent, and he had taken the time to convince the merchants that they and their employees would benefit from it.

The merchants' employees started their training a week after the factory workers completed theirs. Some of the younger employees had already been exposed to the processes at school and had a base of knowledge. Once they completed their training, their bosses assigned them to teams to look into complaints and suggestions.

Much of the criticism, both positive and negative, was directed to specific people and products. The teams used a combination of common sense and statistical data to identify the causes of problems and corrective actions.

Through the suggestion system, Tom's Cafe received numerous complaints about its milkshakes. For one month, owner Tom Rosterman checked almost every milkshake before it was brought out to the customer. However, the customers continued to turn in suggestions for improvement. Tom asked his food quality team to look into the matter. The team members eventually uncovered and corrected the problem. They traced the complaints to Sundays and Mondays, the same days Tom was off. His assistant manager, who took over on those days, was a New York City native who preferred New York style milkshakes — thinner and sweeter — and made them the way he liked — not what local customers demanded.

Joe Carroll's problems at Clover Leaf Motel were much more serious. Carroll was lax in responding to numerous complaints about his dirty rooms and leaky plumbing. More than half of his rooms were usually filled because he had one of only two motels in town. But visitors to Midland City could hardly be impressed with the city's quality products or services if they slept in dirty rooms.

Bill, the five heads of Midland City's manufacturers, and two city council members met for breakfast one morning and decided to give Joe an ultimatum. Either he'd go along with the changes or they'd boycott his motel by recommending to their out-of-town customers and associates that they not stay there.

Joe grudgingly accepted the ultimatum. Bill and his team of manufacturers and council members randomly checked the Clover Leaf for improvement. Joe at first was irritated by the spot checks, but it didn't take him long to learn that the costs of running a clean motel were outweighed by compliments rather than complaints from customers and the resulting increased occupancy. As he finally admitted, "You have to clean eventually so why not do it before someone gets mad."

Suzie's Dress Shop received several complaints through the suggestion system about shoddy merchandise. The complaints took Suzie Harold by surprise, even though she was aware that she was steadily losing customers to stores in Meadan. But she took pride in buying only what she considered quality brands and was surprised by the complaints on quality.

Most of the complaints were vague so she had her sales people interview all the customers who had complained. They asked the customers what they specifically meant by "shoddy product" and why they failed to complain personally to Suzie.

Suzie and her staff finally traced 90 percent of the problems to one culprit — a brand of clothing with seams that more often than not split after only two or three washings. When the customers were asked why they failed to return the garments, they said that they didn't want to make a fuss and that Suzie was a friend.

Suzie realized that her friends had chosen to go elsewhere rather than confront her with a quality problem. For her, it had been an expensive lesson in human behavior.

Suzie approached the manufacturer with no success. "It's your problem to adjust the complaints. We have an image of quality," the manufacturing representative told her. Suzie immediately dropped that product line.

Better communication was the key to a quality image, Suzie decided. She sent a newsletter to her regular customers explaining what the problem had been. "Since our goal is to have only quality merchandise," she wrote, "I want you to *please* let me know whenever you have any problems!"

She decided to offer partial credit to her customers who bought the bad products to compensate them for their loss. Her customers were quite pleased with her honesty and generosity.

Good communication certainly paid off, Suzie concluded as sales began to increase.

All the merchants found using the processes to their benefit. Their employee circles uncovered needed changes in policy, buildings, and, in some cases, training.

Evan Lockwood learned that his dishwasher's backaches were caused by a sink installed four inches too low. Larry Anderson found that he was being taken by out-of-towners because his check cashing rules were too confusing. Sally Severson learned that she could keep her employees happy by just supplying a paper cup dispenser so they could get a drink of water.

The merchants all benefited from the feeling of ownership their employees gained. Teams gave their employees a say in how they did their jobs.

Some of the merchants attended workshops on the other work improvement processes. Many of them felt that they would use work simplification to reduce their paperwork and to optimize their store layouts. They drew on the expertise gained by Midland City Fulfillment in work simplification. The process of change was not the chaos they originally had envisioned. Change was leading them to more customers, more profit, and happier employees.

CHAPTER 17

Trock Plastics: Design of Experiments

Trock Plastics produced a variety of injection molded and compression molded plastic parts. John Trock's father, an expert mold maker, had started the business in the late 1940s and John took over when the elder retired. John, a natural entrepreneur, had tripled his business volume in only eight years.

But for the last two years, his business stabilized with no real growth. Competition was tough and his costs were high.

Pete Ivers at Midland City Machine was one of his best customers. Midland City Machine bought plastic parts for the woodworking tools it manufactured. The two men were close friends as well as dependable business associates.

John had eagerly joined Midland City Machine and the city's three other manufacturers to establish the quality image that Arthur Black and Bill Peterson had envisioned. He and his employees had established quality teams and were using statistical process control. They saw long-term benefits but also saw a lot of short-term confusion as they proceeded with the processes.

The suggestion system had been incorporated at Trock and ideas were flowing into the city-managed system and immediately back to John's staff. He recognized the benefits of the system and set up his own system to handle the suggestions internally to reduce the response time to suggestions.

Three suggestions alone, he found, produced an increase of 2.6 percent in gross profit. The increase was well above what he had anticipated, so he was more than willing to pay the 10 percent of his savings to the city's quality program.

At the strategic planning meeting more than a year before, John had selected the concept of design of experiments as one that he would pioneer in Midland City. He and his foreman, Randy Clark, attended a three-day workshop on the process in Meadan. It was an intensive course, and they devoted many evenings to studying the material after they got back to Midland City.

The instructor had pointed out the need to optimize a product design before it is released for manufacture. That means analyzing all the variables to optimize production and quality at the same time. Design of experiments does just that, the instructor explained. Once in production, statistical process control is the tool to measure and control variation of the product.

Design of experiments, which uses statistics to reduce the costs of experimentation, can be used to optimize interacting variables, the instructor said. He used an example for plastic molding to show the number of variables in a relatively small-scale production process.

INPUT VARIABLE — INJECTION MOLDING

1. Injection time

2. Primary pressure

3. Secondary pressure

4. Screw travel speed

5. Screw rotation speed

6. Mold temperature

7. Hot tip temperature

8. Bond heater temperature

9. Nozzle temperature

10. Cure time

11. Material moisture content

12. Material melt viscosity

Another example involved determining the best ratio of baking powder and baking soda in a cake. With two variables, the normal procedure would be to make four batches of cake with baking powder at the low or high end of the range and with baking soda at the low end of the range. Then two more batches would be run with baking powder at the high end of the range. These four experiments would be needed to gain data to select a best mixture.

Normally engineering schools teach the method of using tests of each combination of variations with one test at the top of the range and one on the bottom. With 12 variables and two tests for each possible combination, the number would be 2^{12} (or two to the 12th power) or 4,096 the instructor explained. If all 4,096 tests were run at a cost of $100 each, the total cost would be $409,600. As a result most industries use a high level of guesswork to determine the optimum combination of variables in a process. Using design of experiments to optimize variables would be much less expensive.

John listened intently as the instructor explained the history of design of experiments, which is sometimes called fractional factorial statistics. It was developed by agriculture scientists in England as a way to limit the number of years of planting needed to produce hybrid seeds. Design of experiments allowed the researchers to limit the number of tests and thus shorten the number of experiments. The result was a reduction in costs and growing years to develop the plants.

Trock and his foreman found the process straightforward but the process was challenging. They knew they would be uncomfortable with the process until they had seen at least a few applications.

At their instructor's recommendation, they bought the book *Design and Analysis of Experiments,* by Douglas C. Montgomery (John Wiley & Sons, 1976), a professor of engineering at the University of Washington, Seattle. They also read some of the writings of Genichi Taguchi, a Japanese leader in process optimization.

Trock Plastics needed to produce error-free plastic parts at the lowest cost possible. John and Randy decided to experiment first with the injection molding for tops of percolator coffee pots. The tops were produced in high volume and were frequently redesigned to change the appearance of the coffee pots.

Every new mold had a number of variables: the shaping of the cavity, the size of the gate, size of vents, etc. The consistency of the plastic, the temperature needed for molding, and the pressure and time needed in the mold were other variables. The company's long-time practice, based on judgment and experience, was to set up the molding press to an estimated best value for each variable. They adjusted variables until they ran parts to specification. Randy had a good feel for this and rarely had much scrap.

They decided to run their first experiment on the current percolator top model. The top ran two shifts five days a week with a 10-cavity mold. John Trock brought in an engineer from Meadan who was experienced in design of experiments. Both John and Randy were still unsure of themselves and happy to have help. The engineer worked for one of their customers who was eager to teach them what he knew.

The engineer said they first needed to gather basic data on how the part was running. He also suggested that they identify the cost savings and cost increases associated with each variable. They started by using data on quality measures from each cavity and on the history of the parts from a quality standpoint.

After they established a range of variance for each variable, they determined a fractional factorial design for the variables affecting their injection process. Those variables were gate size, injection barrel temperature, injection pressure, mold temperature, and cure time.

To find their optimal performance point, they normally would make three runs for each variable: high, medium, and low. With five variables, 243 runs would have been needed. At a cost of $150 per run, that process would have cost $36,450.

But by using design of experiments, they were able to approximate the optimal point in 16 runs at $150 each with a high level of accuracy. Using the process, they spent only $2,400, a savings of $34,100.

They found they could reduce cure time 30 percent by decreasing the mold temperature 10 degrees, decreasing the injection barrel temperature by 15 degrees, increasing the gate size by 18 percent, and increasing pressure by 20 PSI. The total cycle for cure time was normally 40 seconds so the 30 percent decrease reduced the cycle time by 8.4 seconds. The result was an increase in capacity of 21 percent. They produced more product per shift at a lower cost.

John and Randy were amazed at the increase in performance. The new molding parameters also offered more assurance of quality.

"Process optimization can give us a competitive edge both in quality and price," John said to his foreman. "We can keep the company growing."

Another group of John's employees looked at ways to use statistical process control and quality teams. His office staff concentrated on improving order entry and order scheduling functions. One quality team carefully evaluated the causes of error with a cause-and-effect diagram and gathered data on each cause. After the employees finished collecting data, they constructed a Pareto diagram so they could visually identify the major causes of errors. They investigated the major causes to see how they happened and what could be done to prevent them from reoccurring.

His office staff recommended and made several changes:

- They asked for and were given new order forms that ensured completeness and accuracy.
- They requested that sales representatives be briefed on the proper procedures for filling out the forms and on what the costs were if the procedures were not followed.
- They reported all order errors in writing to John and the sales manager and kept cost-of-error data to track the total real cost of each order error. This data was shared weekly with all employees.
- They started a screening procedure using the computer to identify any changes in quantity, part number, or specifications from previous orders.

With the changes, they found they had increased accuracy, reduced errors in the shop, and increased their efficiency in collecting outstanding accounts. Another outcome of the intensive data gathering was the pride generated as the employees' performance increased.

The several office teams in Midland City shared their experiment results. Bill Peterson was glad to hear the enthusiasm with which they reported on their projects and questioned each other for details. These monthly meetings of team leaders and members soon led to publicity in the *Press* with a result of other businesses getting ideas for improvement.

John reported his results with design of experiments at one of the manufacturers' Monday lunch meetings. The executives said they wanted to learn more about the process. Bill agreed to convince the adult education committee to sponsor a training seminar on the process.

Pete Ivers said he wanted to use the process. He was sure that it could help in his painting department where coverage problems and paint runs plagued the appearance of the machine tools he shipped.

"I really feel that we've always been the best quality molders in the state," John told the group. "But now, we have a way to be the most competitive.

"We still have a lot of work ahead of us in training our employees in these new techniques," he continued. "Textbooks will become a part of everyone's evening and weekend reading, and I personally will lead discussion groups. Building more jobs and a new image isn't easy, but it can and will be done."

His testimonial brought a round of applause.

CHAPTER 18

Thirty Months

The day Arthur Black first spoke at the city council meeting seemed like a long time ago for most Midland City residents. They could barely remember what their city was like 30 months before. For most, it had been an active and exciting time of their lives. For some, however, it had been just plain exhausting.

Bill Peterson had been reelected as mayor, with the community threatening to make it a lifetime job. The majority of residents were 100 percent behind Bill and his vision. But Bill knew there were some, including his son, who believed he was leading them in the direction of a lot of work and expense with no assurance of success.

At the Peterson home, discussion during morning coffee and at the dinner table often accelerated to arguments over who in the family was doing more work. But each month saw stronger support for the goals of quality that Midland City and the Peterson family had adopted.

"How's your school work coming along Scott?" Bill asked Scott at the dinner table one evening.

"All right," answered Scott, who had just started his second semester of 11th grade.

"Just 'all right'?" Samantha asked.

"Well, you know we have to work awfully hard and we can't get by with just memorizing things. We really have to understand what we're taught. Our teachers have really gotten tough!"

"It's good for you," said Sarah arrogantly.

Bill frowned at his daughter as a motion to keep her sarcastic comments to herself.

"Doesn't it feel good to really be learning something and not have to fake it?" Bill asked.

"Yeah, but sometimes it hurts my brain to work so hard and sometimes I'm so drained that I can hardly play hockey."

"I doubt that. Nothing will ever stop you from playing hockey," Bill said half jokingly.

Meanwhile, Bill was pleased to find that Midland City's quality tax was a big success. Most businesses readily contributed 10 percent of their net savings that came about because they had successfully used statistical process control, quality circles, team problem solving, the suggestion system, and other quality control processes.

The tax generated more than $350,000 per year. Midland City *Press* reported the savings monthly and covered the deliberations and decisions of the board of advisors in charge of the money.

The advisory board funded several citizen programs to promote quality. An essay contest was held each spring for students in grades six through 12. The students submitted essays regarding the concept of quality improvement and how a community like Midland City could best plan and operate in the future using quality as a guide.

To gather background material for their essays, students visited local factories to observe the processes in action. Parents became involved in planning, proofreading, and sometimes typing the essays. The essays became a family project in many homes.

The essays were judged on how much research and thought they entailed, and if they offered clear, specific, practical, and affordable recommendations. Essays from students in grades six through nine were judged in one category; students in grades 10 through 12 were judged in another.

First-place winners in the younger category were awarded $200, and students who placed first in the older category were awarded $2,000. All second-place winners were awarded $100 and all four third-prize winners were awarded $50. The winning essays were published in the Midland City *Press*.

In addition, if the essays were used and resulted in savings to a business, they would qualify for additional cash awards through the citywide suggestion system.

The first year — the year Sarah won first place for her essay — only a few students entered the competition. But the extensive publicity given to the winners prompted several more entries the following spring. At first editor Terry Brand worried that readers would be bored with the extensive coverage of the essays on the front page. But the publicity actually led to more subscriptions and street sales as relatives proudly bought extra copies that featured their sons, daughters, nieces, nephews, and grandchildren.

The citizen involvement programs emphasized upgrading the overall academic excellence and reputation of Midland City schools. Prior to Arthur Black's speech, National Honor Society meetings were rarely reported in the news, and few residents even remembered the names of past valedictorians. But for nearly two years, academic excellence was promoted much in the same way as athletics were in school and in the Midland City *Press*.

Students with a B average or better began wearing academic patches on their school jackets. Honor students held three meetings each school year featuring pizza, pop, and a special interest speaker. Students with C averages and who were showing significant improvement also were invited. The meetings proved to be an excellent way to involve marginal students in the quest for quality. Many average students found that being a part of the "brain trust" wasn't so bad after all and began to see the benefits of striving for National Honor Society standards.

The committee in charge of improving test grades provided transportation for honor students to the state university in Meadan and to plants in the city where they could explore career interests.

The names of honor students and students who were rapidly improving their grades were published after each school semester in Midland City *Press*.

At the end of spring semester, photographs of all honor students of the year were a front page feature in the newspaper.

Juniors and seniors were encouraged to work for at least a month in their career interest areas at local businesses. The committee subsidized the students' salaries to inspire the local businesses to hire the short-term student employees. The students had to write reports on their experience and they rated the businesses according to how well it contributed to their career interest. The reports were graded and the students with the best reports presented them at all school assemblies.

Superintendent Helen Sikorski noticed that grades were rapidly improving and many of the discipline problems dissolved as more and more students took advantage of the programs. She anticipated a continuing rise in SAT scores as the younger students moved into high school.

The emphasis on helping Midland City grow was becoming an obsession with many.

With the money generated from the quality tax, Midland City had been able to send several travel teams to seminars and on tours of manufacturers and organizations that used quality improvement processes. The team members were selected carefully and the numbers were kept low. They shared what they had learned in presentations at businesses and at the schools, and acted as consultants and advisers to the committee members.

Bill was pleased with how eager the manufacturers and organizations in other cities were to share information with Midland City. Most were impressed by how the entire community was moving toward a goal of a quality product for everyone.

After a few trips, Bill realized that the data gathering, particularly in Meadan, provided not only ideas for Midland City but also served as advertisement about what his community was doing. Two common questions from many outside Midland City were: "How is Midland City doing it? And how can you measure it?" Those people were especially impressed with how much money had been saved and the 10 percent quality tax that then yielded more than $350,000 annually.

Some large manufacturers in Meadan were using just-in-time (JIT) inventory management and total quality control (TQC). As Bill and the council members reviewed the processes, they felt they had identified the next phase for Midland City.

Bill was well aware that he and his people could learn about JIT and TQC by going to Japan, where the processes are used extensively. But he was convinced Midland City would benefit more by studying manufacturers in the United States and Canada, preferably present or potential customers, who used the processes.

Midland City established "Commitment Day" 24 months after Black's first speech in Midland City. The day was devoted to Midland City residents who had shown their commitment to quality. The first year, there was a citywide barbecue in Bingle Park. In the afternoon, the committees presented reports on their accomplishments and their future plans. Terry Brand arranged for a special issue of the *Press* to commemorate the day with photographs of the committees and articles of their accomplishments.

Arthur Black, who was the honored guest, lavishly praised Midland City and said he was amazed at how rapidly it had improved product quality as well as its local economy. Bill and the city council members presented Black with a plaque with the inscription: "Key to quality — Midland City."

"You're absolutely right," Black responded with pleasure. "Quality is the key to every city."

That evening, two bands performed — a rock band for the young people and a country western band for the older residents. Fireworks topped off the celebration.

The next year, Midland City had a similar program with Black as guest speaker again. The winners of the essay contest read their essays during the afternoon ceremony, and a parade was featured with prizes for volunteer marchers who created a winning banner or costume bearing a slogan of quality.

As they planned the third annual "Commitment Day," Bill and his committee members decided to focus on drawing state and national attention to Midland City's accomplishments. By all measures, the local manufacturers were producing quality products. Both Trock Plastics and Star Electronics had achieved certified vendor status by their customers in Meadan, meaning their manufacturing processes were under statistical control to the level that their customers were guaranteed quality and could use the parts on their assembly lines without inspections.

Bill felt it was time to publicize what he liked to call "the miracle of Midland City." He knew publicity would focus many envious eyes on Midland City and fan the fires of competition. But keeping the accomplishments secret would not benefit Midland City.

He asked State Senator Randy Anderson to pursue national recognition for Midland City by nominating its four manufacturers for the Productivity Award established by the president of the United States. The award is eagerly sought by large manufacturers because it recognizes recipients as being among the "100 best" in the nation.

The city council members established the Arthur Black Medal to present to the city's outstanding two quality teams. They had the medals mounted on plaques for the office or home and reproduced them in pin size for personal wearing. The two teams were rewarded also with all-expense-paid trips to the convention on team problem solving or statistical techniques of their choice.

To gain additional prestige, Midland City hosted a day-long conference on quality and productivity techniques, featuring Arthur Black and several nationally known speakers. Mailings on the conference were sent out nationwide through memberships of the American Society for Quality Control, the American Society for Performance Improvement, the National Association of Manufacturers, the National Chamber of Commerce, and other professional organizations.

The conference was a big project for a relatively small community. But the committee members worked hard to attract the top names in productivity and quality processes.

Midland City residents were proud to host a national conference — the publicity was a big plus for the local merchants and manufacturers. The flyers printed for the conference cited examples of their accomplishments.

During the conference, a display area featured examples of the merchants' and manufacturers' parts and products impacted by statistics, circles, and the citywide suggestion system. The circle members were on hand to explain their successes. Midland City Machine's new lathe was a popular example.

A citywide cultural change had taken place in the brief 30 months, Bill explained to Rainville Mayor Ralph Huber during a round of golf in Rainville. Bill hadn't played golf for weeks because he had been so busy — he felt great to be back on the course. He was headed for a 40, he thought.

"The entire city has lined up behind the change process to make our community a growing one, not a dying one," Bill explained to Huber as they walked to the second hole. "The process of understanding is part of the family, school, and business structure. It has become a fundamental part of life in Midland City. Even those who are not vocal supporters have contributed."

"But how do you know for sure?" Huber asked.

"We see it in class assignments and projects, in our suggestion system, in our circles and problem-solving teams, and at our annual picnics in the park," Bill answered.

Mayor Huber had difficulty understanding how Bill convinced his community to stand behind him.

"They all realized that what I was trying to do was for them, and now they are taking the initiative. The secret has been communication and recognition," Bill told him. He explained how every successful organization needs to offer its employees a feeling of ownership and recognition, and rewards for their work.

"Terry Brand has been a godsend for publishing our plans and achievements, and there have been several newsletters started in our companies and schools to recognize good employees. Our team meetings provide another method for sharing data. All this is supported by the local grapevine that carries news at an unbelievable rate."

He explained how most businesses in Midland City offered cash rewards for usable ideas for improvement that came through the citywide suggestion system. Other rewards for good ideas were emerging through a number of profit sharing or gain sharing programs. Some companies offered preferential parking spots to those employees who submitted good ideas, he said. The cash rewards for essay contests and for outstanding teams also encouraged performance.

"We still have a long way to go, but we've come a long way."

Bill golfed his best game ever — a 35, one under par.

CHAPTER 19

Japan: Just-in-Time and Total Quality Control

The three years since the strategic planning meeting had yielded results beyond Bill Peterson's wildest dreams. Every business that had used the quality control processes had profited, and the citywide suggestion system had induced millions of dollars in savings. Some businesses were even reopening.

Still, Bill wasn't entirely convinced that sending a study team to Japan was in the best interest of Midland City. He knew the city could afford to send only a few people, and the average folks of Midland City wouldn't be chosen. He was afraid that a city-paid trip to Japan would be seen as a city-paid boondoggle for a selected few at the expense of an unselected many.

However, with the farm economy still on the decline, he knew Midland City had to find a way to create more jobs for farm families. He contacted various groups that worked with manufacturers seeking ideal rural locations. The organizations gave him the names of several manufacturers that had recently located in small communities across the country.

He conducted an informal survey of 25 manufacturers asking them what Midland City could do to better position itself for offers.

"We want our potential managers knowledgeable in just-in-time inventory management and total quality control," all of the manufacturers answered.

Fifteen of the manufacturers said they would seriously consider locating a plant in Midland City if its leaders were knowledgeable in and had offered their workers training in the two processes. Several of the manufacturers strongly suggested that Bill take a study team to Japan to witness the processes in action.

With enough convincing from the manufacturers and city council members, Bill changed his mind. "The time is ripe for a Japan excursion. We have the need and good reason," he announced at a council meeting.

The week after Bill agreed to the trip, Midland City *Press* featured an article, at Bill's suggestion, about the results of the surveys and comments from the 15 manufacturers. The article addressed Midland City's need for more jobs for farm families, and quoted Bill's explanation of how the city could prosper by sending a study team to Japan. In the article, Bill asked for volunteers to help choose the study team members and to help plan the Japan itinerary.

Once again, Bill called Arthur Black for guidance. Black could offer invaluable advice because he had been to Japan several times.

In less than a week, 22 residents volunteered to help plan the trip. After only two weeks the council agreed on who would go. At Black's advice, they chose 10 people who represented a variety of occupations because the team members would visit a variety of businesses from manufacturing plants to insurance companies, and would meet with Kaoru Ishikawa, Ryuji Fukuda, Shigeo Shingo, and other key consultants on quality enhancement processes.

They chose Bill; Helen Sikorski; Pete Ivers; John Trock; Randy Clark; Bill Willis, an engineer at Midland City Tool and Die; Betty Jacobs, a quality engineer at Midland City Manufacturing; John Hammer, a machinist at Midland City Machine; Norma Dahl, an office circle leader at Star Electronics; and Cheryl Jones, a quality circle facilitator at Midland City Fulfillment.

During their first meeting, a week after they were chosen, Black briefed them on Japan's economic history.

"Much of Japan's modern posture began with the Emperor Meiji," Black began. "Meiji and other leaders, no more than 50 in all, began the original great cultural revolution in 1868. Before that, Japan had no modern business or industry."

Meiji led the first major change in 1868. General Douglas MacArthur started the second major change in 1945 when he introduced statistical process control, value analysis, work flow analysis, and other quality control processes developed in the United States.

World War II left Japan with a bombed out industrial base and a nation with no real goals. The emperor-controlled government was gone and American forces had occupied their land. It was a nation unable to feed itself or keep warm on its own. The country desperately needed export income to buy food and fuel. Most of the world remembered a prewar Japan that exported cheap copies or inexpensive low quality goods.

General MacArthur directed change in many aspects of Japanese life. He helped change the school system to provide quality education. He brought in Deming, Juran, and other consultants to teach Japanese management how to control quality. In a sense, MacArthur and his people humanized Japan, Black said. While the democracy preachers of the U.S. occupation pushed for the basic dignity of the individual, U.S. corporations told the Japanese businessmen that they were running their businesses wrong and advised them on how to work more efficiently.

"The U.S. corporations told the Japanese that they had too many financial men running their companies," Black explained. "They told them that they had too much bureaucracy, and they were paying too little attention to the production man on the factory floor and the quality of their products."

"Sound familiar?" he asked. "Well, the Japanese made use of that criticism and turned things around."

Black explained how Deming worked with the Japan Union of Scientists and Engineers (JUSE) to establish the concept of statistical measurement and team problem solving.

Team problem solving was easy for the Japanese — their national tendency is to work in groups. Statistics, however, was new and posed quite a challenge. But they readily accepted the challenge. Japan's success didn't happen overnight, Black stressed. The Japanese worked vigorously from 1947 to 1977 before they perfected the processes that now dominate their production.

"But take note of Japan's lack of focus in such areas as merchandise distribution and agriculture," Black said. "In these areas, the country is far behind the U.S. I want you to observe the good ideas without feeling that success is unique to Japan.

"Also, you must distinguish between mechanical and cultural differences in Japan. The U.S. can adapt most of Japan's mechanical processes, but many of the cultural persuasions are not suited for our use. Teamwork is one that we can learn to use. The problems of women and minorities in Japan are examples of where the Japanese culture is far behind ours. Also, Japanese employees are not free to move from company to company like we are here."

Black had several contacts in the Japan Management Association, a prestigious organization in Japan with a central staff of hundreds of people who analyze industry trends and provide training and guidance to Japanese businesses. He said the association would be willing to help plan and schedule the team's meetings and tours in Japan.

The study team members met with Black every other Tuesday evening for three months until they finished planning their itinerary.

Meanwhile, Midland City's citizens' reactions were mixed. Most people truly supported the trip, but a few scoffed at the idea and called it "the boondoggle of the year." To avoid further objection, the team members reluctantly decided against extending their stay in Japan for sightseeing. They also agreed not to bring their spouses, even on their own expense.

Black reassured the team members that going to Japan was the best way to further study the processes. They would return to Midland City more knowledgeable in the processes than most American business presidents, he said.

The team, he stressed, had a good agenda. However, he warned, the Japanese companies rarely have women working in high-ranking positions, thus some of the companies could find it uncomfortable having to work with the women team members.

"I'm not suggesting that you change the makeup of the team," he clarified.

"Just be aware that your hosts may be uncomfortable and act accordingly."

The day the team departed couldn't have been more perfect. The sun was shining and there was a fresh blanket of snow on the ground. The weather in Japan for the week, they were told, would be delightful, but cold.

Few people other than their families and close friends traveled to Meadan to see them off at the airport. Samantha and several of the husbands and other wives brought their cameras to Meadan to record the departure. After all, it was the first trip to Japan for the 10 team members.

Bill wished Arthur Black could come along, but he knew he was fully capable of taking the lead.

The study team members hired an interpreter to serve as a guide, even though many of the larger Japanese companies had people competent in English. In keeping with Japanese tradition, they brought small gifts to present to their hosts at each company.

The 14-hour plane ride was exhausting. The team members spent much of the time talking with the interpreter about what their week-long stay in Japan would be like.

They arrived at Narita Airport in Tokyo at 3:00 p.m. on Sunday. The taxi ride to the Capitol Tokyu Hotel in the Akasaka district was interesting. The taxi drivers drove faster than most New York cab drivers, and each cab was equipped with a door release lever that the cab driver controlled from the front seat. Bill, not understanding that he was to exit from the door that the cab driver had opened, exited the car on the opposite side — the traffic side — and received a citation. He learned the hard way that getting out of a car on the traffic side is illegal in Japan.

The team members were pleased to find the Capitol Tokyu Hotel conveniently located near subway lines and with plenty of shopping and restaurants nearby. But they were disappointed in how expensive everything was. The food prices were frightening: $20 for a plain hamburger! But the restaurants, as were all Japanese public places, were impeccably clean.

They traveled to most of the plants by train and subway, the least expensive and fastest means of travel.

The five days of meetings and presentations passed quickly. Each evening the team members met after dinner to share what they had learned and to sharpen their lists of questions for the next day.

They attended a briefing on Japanese quality control. Bill previously had read much about the Japanese process in two books. One, *Study of Toyota Production System,* by Shigeo Shingo, identifies the processes leading to just-in-time and the problems Japanese manufacturers faced in starting statistical process control. The other *Guide to Quality Control,* by Kaoru Ishikawa, details statistical process control methods and is considered a basic business textbook in Japan and America.

Ishikawa promotes a Plan — Do — Check — Action Control Cycle as the sequence of action to follow in process improvement. Japanese quality

CONTROL CIRCLE

control calls for company-wide quality control through education and training in quality control, quality circles, quality circle audits, statistical methods, and a nationwide promotion of quality control activities. The team members were already familiar with the six quality improvement steps, which were almost exactly what they had done at Arthur Black's direction.

"I've noticed a continuing indication of total quality control," Bill said after a visit to a plant that had done exceedingly well with Japanese quality control. "Each operator is responsible for the quality of his product, and each operator has the training, tools, and inspection equipment to do the job right the first time. I can see how with the right quality checks final inspection can be done essentially in an audit mode with a limited number of people."

The team members kept careful notes for Terry Brand who would prepare a "Japan Diary" for the paper after they returned to Midland City. They were disappointed that several of the plants would not allow cameras. In addition to the diary, they planned to produce a trip report and slide presentation. They took special note of the cleanliness and neatness in the factories, stores, restaurants, hotels, and trains. Japan is the size of Montana with a population that equals half of the U.S. population, the interpreter pointed out. Because it is so crowded, Japan has to keep things exceedingly neat.

Almost every factory they visited used just-in-time inventory or the KANBAN concept, which calls for producing parts only as fast as they are needed. Just-in-time eliminates the costs of inventory stockpiling and the risks of large rework or scrap costs due to error. A measure repeatedly used in Japan is the days of work in process (WIP).

Poka-yoke, the team members learned, is a concept of error-proofing a machine or assembly or office operation. Shigeo Shingo originated the process. Many Japanese manufacturers have used poka-yoke for years. It requires running a completed product through tests, measurements, or inspections that become an automatic measure to test and assure the product is correct.

Japanese companies used single minute exchange of dies (SMED) to allow rapid change of tooling in all types of machines. The rapid change cuts down on lost time during tool change, allowing a better control of quality with less inventory because runs are efficiently reduced. SMED is considered a fundamental process before starting just-in-time.

Helen Sikorski liked the way the Japanese quality circles operated. She felt her teachers would too, although they probably would not favor meeting 25 percent of the time on company time and 75 percent on their own time as most of the quality circles in Japan do. Maybe they would, she thought, if they were rewarded for their work as the Japanese quality circles are. Many Japanese circle members receive a cash stipend of $10 when they've completed a report or study. The report then enters a competition series. Winners are rewarded with a trip to an all-Japan conference and a Japan Union of Scientists and Engineers sponsored ocean cruise to Hong Kong or a trip to Hawaii.

The Japanese effectively staff and promote circle training, the team members learned. One company they visited had five promotion specialists and 10 trainers for 1,300 hourly and 2,200 salaried employees.

The team members were amazed at how effective the Japanese suggestion systems worked. All companies had suggestion systems: some had ones to generate ideas only, some had value analysis systems, and others used them to generate both ideas and solutions. With up to 100 suggestions per employee each year, the participation rate in Japan was 50 times higher than Midland City's.

Awards included value awards up to $1 for each idea submitted, but awards up to $5,000 were possible for the best ideas. Tangible ideas were evaluated against a matrix of value of savings, creativity, and originality as measures.

The team members were especially interested in how the Japanese companies used statistical process control. All Japanese employees are trained in the process, and it is used as part of their circle or suggestion system involvement.

The team members were not surprised to learn that the Japanese are heavily involved in sampling inspection and supplier certification. Operators do most of their own inspections regularly during production as well as after new setups. They use poka-yoke (automated inspection devices) to check dimensions. The members team saw no $\overline{X}$ and R charts — charts with plots of measurements — in any of the plants. The Japanese, they learned, feel the costs to maintain the charts are too high compared to their effectiveness and rely on poka-yoke or 100 percent mechanical inspection and operator inspection. The Japanese plot statistical data only when starting new products or when problems arise. The team members did see some quality charts showing .002 percent error on complex assemblies — the Japanese obviously had their processes in control.

The manufacturers had built quality right into the design process of every part. They focused on making the designs easy to inspect as well as easy to build and operate by using detailed quality analysis and establishing critical parameters to measure. Design of experiments and Taguchi analysis were both used to optimize designs and production processes.

John Trock was especially interested in how Japanese managers motivated their employees to take active roles in the processes. The managers provided much direction and required detailed reporting and measuring of the processes successes and failures. Several used company slogans to focus activity on specific goals for the month, quarter, or year.

Several of the Japanese managers commented on impact the United States' focus on high asset returns had on U.S. businesses. The United States seeks a 25 percent return on investments, while Japan seeks 5 percent. The focus on high returns reduces investment, increases labor costs, and results in higher product costs, they said.

Bill noted that Japanese businesses, to their advantage, spend a higher percentage of assets than their U.S. counterparts do on robotics and automation. The auto company they had visited was particularly impressive. But in some plants they saw machine lines that were obsolete or exceeded capacity needs by 10 to 1. Excess steel and shipbuilding in Japan are examples of planning problems, he said. Japan, they saw, was not perfect at everything.

The Japanese managers complained about the high costs of doing business in the United States. They blamed the costs on an increasing number of legal concerns with each business transaction, soaring costs of product liability, and employee lawsuits.

The team members pointed out the high cost of living in Japan. The cost of housing, fuel, food, and clothing are too high, they said. And factory workers salaries are about one fourth less than they are in the United States, while the engineers and managers in Japan make about one half as much as their counterparts in America.

"We are lucky to be living in a country rich in natural resources and cropland, and capable of exporting most commodities," said Betty Jacobs. "Japan has to import almost 50 percent of its food, plus all energy and most raw materials."

"Americans must work harder and produce better quality products for their salaries if they want to keep them," said Pete Ivers. He quoted Arthur Black: "America is changing — either we manage change or change manages us."

By Friday night, the team members were exhausted. They had learned a great deal and had enjoyed their stay, but they were ready to go home to their families.

They spent much of Saturday taking in the Japanese culture. They rode the bullet train to Mount Fuji and had lunch there. The beautiful Shinto Shrine next to their hotel was one of their favorite sights. That evening they went to the Ginza for shopping and dinner. They all bought gifts for their families. Some had grown so accustomed to the fresh kimonos provided in their rooms daily at the Capitol Tokyu that they bought kimonos to bring home.

The 5,950 mile flight on Sunday seemed to go much faster than it had a week before because most of the team members slept for nearly the entire 14 hours. Even Bill, who could barely wait to try out tempura cooking on his family, fell asleep an hour into the flight.

CHAPTER 20

The Lead

Midland City *Press* published the "Japan Diary" the Thursday after the study team returned home. The article was picked up by the Associated Press and it was run in the Meadan City *Tribune* that Sunday.

Bill Peterson couldn't have asked for more. The following week, the state coordinator for Apex Corporation called. She said she had read the article in the *Tribune* and wanted to know more about Midland City, including how many available workers it had. Bill decided to keep the inquiry quiet until it progressed to something more concrete. He didn't want to raise everyone's hopes, and he especially didn't want to stir up competition from other communities. Carter, only 60 miles away, had started to follow in Midland City's footsteps, and Bill didn't want Mayor Cohen to get wind of this too early.

Bill was confident that Midland City residents would welcome Apex and could supply the corporation with a host of exceptional employees. Most of his people were knowledgeable in quality control processes and had some experience in implementing many of them. Midland City would be a tough competitor in the contest for the Apex plant. He promptly provided the Apex representatives with the survey data that he had collected the year before on available workers. According to the survey, Midland City had more than 500 people looking for work, many of whom were only marginally employed on farms.

He and the city council members prepared a formal proposal on why Apex would benefit from locating a plant in Midland City. They sent the proposal along with the additional survey information to the Apex state coordinator.

Council member Dean Ostman continued to pursue other manufacturers, while Bill and the other city council members pooled their energies to win the Apex plant. Teamwork and dedication were really beginning to pay off.

CHAPTER 21

Reaching Out

Bill was becoming a celebrity, and he enjoyed every minute of it. He was cast in the limelight with Apex Corporation's announcement that Midland City was among the four finalists for a plant location. Several cities across the state and in other states invited him to speak about Midland City's success.

Most of his audiences lacked training in statistical process control, quality circles, and the other improvement processes, just as Midland City residents had in the beginning. But his audiences had a common bond: They were threatened with the possibility of losing something important to them — something that would deteriorate if their communities failed to change.

In each community, there was a wide range of threat felt, much like there had been in Midland City. Many were like Bill, whose garage was somewhat cushioned from the changing economy. But many were like the implement dealer, who had to shut his doors.

Bill usually arranged his speeches around four points: a vision, an imperative, a process, and a plan. He sounded much like Arthur Black, but Bill really could speak from the heart using Midland City as the ultimate example.

He usually started talking about the *imperative* by insisting that his audiences understand the global threat caused by the United States' huge trade deficit. "Anyone will run into problems if he or she spends more than they have," he said. He usually used anecdotes relative to local or state issues to describe the problem.

TRADE BALANCES

$ in billions

	1982	1983	1984	1985	1986
United States	−36	−61	−111	−135	−124
Canada	+15	+15	+16	+16	+5
Japan	+18	+32	+42	+49	+83

Bill usually used Midland City as the *vision*. He enjoyed watching the excitement grow among his audiences as he traced the four years leading up to the Apex proposal. Many people could see the benefits but few really understood the community-wide dedication vital to success.

To explain the *process,* he used Arthur Black's chart of how a factory works (see p. 15). The management responsibilities, he would say, are tied into a community. The key is for the community and management to agree on the processes to be taught and used. "Midland City was fortunate to have Arthur Black's guidance," he repeated often. "Our focus on statistical process control and quality circles really worked."

"But training is only the start," he stressed. Bill, who played a trumpet in high school, would often compare trumpet training to training in

PHASES OF TRAINING

Training a Trumpet Player	SPC Transformation of a Worker
What the valves do	Understanding of SPC
Learn to play a scale	Learn basic statistics
Learn to play a tune	Learn to apply statistics to your job
Become part of a band	Use statistics in a circle environment
Perform complex music	Support broad problem solving initiatives
Graduate	Transfer/promotion/retirement

statistical process control. "You have to learn how to apply what you have learned and know what tools to use for the desired outcomes."

The *plan* was something that each community could own and accept, Bill told his audiences. But people would have to learn to change.

"You must learn to be problem finders and diagnosticians, and learn to formulate theories and conduct experiments," he told his audiences. "You must understand what you can and cannot do, have your authorities' support and respect, both financially and philosophically, and be recognized and rewarded for your work."

One of the risks, though, is the classic management attitude in America, he continued. Management has to be willing to spend the time and money

---

MANAGEMENT

- Learns how simple the SPC process really can be.

- Is reluctant to spend any more time and money than necessary.

- Ignores the long-established culture and the inherent resistance to change.

- Assumes an "edict" will achieve compliance and resulting change of culture.

- Has a record in America of repeated failure to cause change.

---

for training, recognize established cultures and inherent resistance to change in their companies, and promote change with positive reinforcement.

His final visual, *How to Succeed,* was aimed at community and business leaders.

HOW TO SUCCEED

- Select the process best for your operation.

- Establish skills training relevant to each worker group.

- Insist that process be used and that ALL reports contain evidence of process use.

- Include in your directives evidence of your involvement in using the process.

- Have continuous training to expand knowledge of process techniques.

  Consultants • Speakers • Videotapes • Employee Success Stories
  Awards • Programs • Conference Participation

"Quality must become your way of life," he would say as he closed his presentations.

In four years, Bill had emerged as the "Arthur Black" to a whole new audience. The revival of Midland City coupled with his reputation as the mayor who instigated change, spurred audiences everywhere to accept the points he made.

It wouldn't be too long before the leaders of other revived communities would be preaching change to others.

At home, life was never better. Sarah was in her second year of college on an academic scholarship, and Scott, a high school senior with a B average, had hockey scholarship offers from three universities.

"I'll never be a brain like you Dad, but it sure feels good to try," Scott confided in his father one morning.

"You never can tell," Bill reassured his son. "Look how far you've come in only four years."

Appendices

This section contains selected descriptions and reference materials to help you better understand how the processes used in *Midland City* work. The materials were also selected to provide a vision as to how you could use these processes and help you select a starting point and a path to follow for your city.

I chose to provide details on only two of the processes since there is limited room in one book. I have provided references to authors who treat all of these processes.

This section contains:

1. **Team problem solving/quality circles** This is an expanded description of the process. This process provides the needed team approach to problem solving.

2. **Suggestion system** This is also an expanded description. This process is easy to install and allows participation by everyone.

3. **Pictorial charts** on the operation of a variety of processes*:

   Cause-and-Effect Diagram with Cards (CEDAC)
   Design of Experiments
   Ergonomics
   Input/Output Analysis
   Just-in-Time Manufacturing (JIT)
   Nominal Group Technique (NGT)
   Statistical Process Control (SPC)
   Team Building
   Value Engineering/Value Analysis (VE/VA)
   Visual Controls
   Work Flow Analysis

4. **Nominal group technique**

5. **Performance improvement process** flowchart.*

6. **Performance measurement process** description and examples of performance measurement in a variety of business situations.*

7. **Glossary** This is an expanded glossary providing a summary of the process and data on books and training available.

---

*Reprinted or adapted from "A Performance Improvement Guide," Honeywell Inc. MRC 4-86-4.

Team Problem Solving/Quality Circles*

In *Midland City,* I have labeled the employee groups as teams rather than circles. To me, the terms are synonymous and *Midland City* could have been written either way.

Quality circles, as a title for team problem solving, has fallen into disfavor to the point that the International Association of Quality Circles (IAQC) has been renamed to the Association for Quality and Participation. It is in recognition of this trend that this book uses team problem solving.

The term, quality circles, is alive and well in Japan. Their quality circles are the primary form of team problem solving. The term is still accepted and used in many businesses in the United States. However, the quality circle process was so abused by management in many companies that it is not acceptable by either workers or management.

The following materials detail quality circles and how the process works. I did not modify this material since quality circles are team problem solving.

The Quality Circles Movement

To understand the quality circles movement, one must consider the origin and development of the quality control circles (QCC) concept. Leading up to the initiation of the first QCCs (of which there were three) in Japan in 1962 were 12 years of preparation. In 1949, the Union of Japanese Scientists and Engineers (JUSE) invited W. Edwards Deming, of the United States, to teach statistical methods to Japanese industry. Deming based his approach on his experience with American industry, where the use of statistical methods had not spread beyond manufacturing departments. When given the opportunity to teach statistical methods to Japanese industry, Deming stressed the importance of using statistical methods *throughout* the organization, from the time the product is designed and materials are procured until a product is in the hands of the consumer.

In 1950, Deming assured 50 top Japanese executives that if they used statistical methods, they would be producing the finest quality of products in the world within five years. Within four years changes such as the following occurred:

- One manufacturer reduced the rework on wire to 10 percent of what it had been previously.
- A steel company reduced coal consumption per ton of steel by 28 percent.
- A pharmaceutical company tripled production on one of its products using the same machinery and the same number of workers.

*Reprinted with permission from "Quality Circles: Applications in Vocational Education," by Russell F. Lloyd and Virgil R. Rehg. Ohio State University: The National Center for Research in Vocational Education, IN 249, 1983.

Deming (1981) defines the forces that came together to cause the explosion in quality and productivity as follows: JUSE, statistical knowledge, the instructing of engineers, and conferences with top management. In 1962, a fifth force was added: QCCs. QCCs were the outgrowth of a long-used Japanese social custom, Kaoru Ishikawa (1980) formalized Japan's traditional group method and brought it to management's attention, along with the important contributions the groups were making in the improvement of work processes.

By 1954, the use of statistical methods was well-known throughout Japan, but Japanese top management was far from being conscious of the importance of quality. Joseph Juran (1952), a management consultant from the United States, was then invited to Japan. In his work there, he emphasized the importance of making quality control an integral part of management, practicing it in the total context of management improvement. In his *Quality Control Handbook,* Juran (1952) called this concept "total quality control" (TQC).

Between 1955 and 1960, Japan experienced a significant growth of TQC throughout industry. In some companies, however, it took 15 years to achieve TQC. The Japanese concept of TQC calls for everyone in the organization, from top management to hourly workers, to be knowledgeable of statistical quality control methods and to participate jointly in the upgrading of company-wide quality control practices. The Japanese now call this company-wide quality control (CWQC).

The growth of the Japanese QC movement since 1960 has been phenomenal. There are now over 100,000 quality circles registered with JUSE, and there are thought to be six to 10 times that number, in addition, that are not registered (Ouchi 1981). Since each QC is comprised of approximately 10 members, as many as 11 million workers are involved in the QC movement throughout Japan. It is quite apparent that Japan is now the world's leader in productivity growth, and in one generation Japanese industry has been transformed from the producer of inferior products to that of superior products. Japanese management made quality its number one priority and continues to enjoy the benefits of that commitment.

Quality Circles Outside of Japan

The growth of the QC movement outside of Japan began in the 1960s as news of Japanese success spread. Most of the early adoption of QC concepts occurred in the Far East: Taiwan, Korea, Singapore, Malaysia, Hong Kong, and the Philippines. In the Western world, Brazil was the first country where QCs were implemented. Today there are few industrialized countries where QCs are not being used, and industries in all of the world's industrialized countries have shown interest in implementing the process.

In the United States, the QC concept was first implemented by the Lockheed Company's Missile and Space Division. In 1972, a group of

Lockheed personnel visited Japan to study the QC process and discuss the concept with Japanese managers. Convinced that the process would work, they purchased training materials, hired a facilitator, and formed a small department with the responsibility for implementing the concept. The QC process was implemented in 1974, and within two years 30 quality circles had been formed. A $500,000 investment in the program has resulted in estimated savings of $3 million.

The Lockheed success was widely publicized. The spread of the concept to other U.S. companies was slow, however, until three individuals who were experienced with quality circles left Lockheed to implement QCs throughout the country. Today there are over 1,500 private sector organizations that have some form of the QC process in operation. Unlike Japan, where most QCs are in manufacturing, many of those in the United States are made up of white-collar workers in service, engineering, and other nonmanufacturing areas.

European companies have been slow in adopting the QC process. England, Sweden, and the Netherlands were the first countries where QCs were formed — in the 1970s. In France, quality circles first appeared in 1980, and by the end of 1981, over 100 organizations had implemented them. Some organizations in Italy, Norway, Poland, Finland, and West Germany also have implemented QCs.

It is evident that a worldwide revolution in management has occurred. The Japanese initiated this dramatic change through the diligent application of statistical quality control principles, the adoption of the TQC philosophy, and the use of the quality control circles process. A greater commitment to quality than to short-term profits has resulted in increased productivity, a larger share of the world market, and — ultimately — greater profits.

Quality Circles in the United States

One of the newest productivity-enhancing techniques on the American scene, the QC concept, is described as follows (Katzell and associates 1977):

> This technique offers a significant potential for tapping the wealth of imagination and ingenuity that lies within each worker. Called "quality circles," it provides an environment for active participation of employees in areas of problem recognition and analysis, together with implementation of corrective measures.

The QC concept attempts to combine several organizational interventions developed in the behavioral sciences into one process that recognizes, involves, and develops the creative intelligence of workers. The QC concept in action is often referred to as a quality of work life or an organization development program. Confusion about these three terms is common, probably because of their similarities. Thus, an attempt to define them is in order.

Quality of work life (QWL) is a generic term that refers to the objectives of organization development strategies. Specifically, it includes employees' perceptions about their work and work environment. The QC concept is implemented so that the QWL can be improved. Organization development (OD), on the other hand, is a field of study in its own right — a subdiscipline of applied social psychology. Originating from the behavioral sciences, it includes many concepts that have application in the organizational context. A variety of practical strategies for effecting changes in organizations has, in turn, evolved. The sum total of these socio-psychological theories, along with the strategies for introducing them, is organization development. One of the strategies available to the OD consultant is the QC concept.

OD is a widely divergent field and one that is variously conceptualized. A useful conceptual framework was developed by Leavitt (1965) and later modified by Friedlander and Brown (1974). It views organizations as being composed of: (1) people who have varying sets of values, styles, and skills; (2) technologies with varying characteristics; and (3) varying processes and structures, each reflecting different kinds of relationships between people or between people and their work. Friedlander and Brown's conceptualization of OD speaks to the need for change in the technology and structure (technostructural change) and/or change in individuals and their interaction processes (human-processual change), rather than an attempt to change only the people, only the structure, or only the technology of the organization.

Human-processual change and technostructural change each have their own approaches, and these approaches converge at the interface of the organizational process and structure. The technostructural approach to organization development includes interventions (i.e., strategies for change, such as job enlargement and job enrichment) into the technology and structure of the organization. The human-processual approach to organization development, on the other hand, includes interventions affecting individuals as they interact with other individuals (intra- and intergroup), with technology, or with structure. The QC concept is a human-processual approach to organization development.

Quality Circles

QCs are comprised of small groups of employees who voluntarily meet on a regular basis to identify, analyze, and develop solutions to problems, and to implement those solutions when feasible. This definition may be further clarified by a description of the common elements of quality circles — size, voluntarism, meetings, tool skills, and problem-solving methodology.

Size

Quality circles typically range in size between three and 15 employees, with the preferred size being at least five and no more than 10 members. If the group is too small, the interaction among group members tends to be limited, resulting in a scarcity of ideas. If the group exceeds 10 members, individuals are not usually afforded sufficient opportunities to participate, leading to apathy and disinterest.

Voluntarism

Workers typically are afforded freedom of choice in joining a QC. This freedom is an initial indication that management is committed to the concept. It is an indication both of how well management understands the QC philosophy and how deeply into the managerial structure the understanding has penetrated. When QCs are implemented on a voluntary basis, their achievements and benefits have a positive effect on the entire organization (given that the process has been properly implemented otherwise). The ultimate goal, of course, is that the QC process will become a way of life in the work place.

Meetings

A weekly one-hour QC meeting is the rule, but there are exceptions, of course. Established QCs sometimes meet less often because subcircle meetings are held to discuss progress during information collection, solution development, or some other phase of the problem-solving process. Decisions about the meeting schedule and location provide management with an opportunity to demonstrate commitment. Meetings should always be held as scheduled. Frequent postponement of meetings communicates to workers that QCs are not important. This also applies to the meeting location. QCs must have a suitable place to meet and must be provided with necessary supplies.

Tool Skills

During the problem-solving process, several tool skills are used by QC members. These are described by Deming (1981) and Ishikawa (1981) as "simple statistical" tool skills. They can be subdivided into two categories: basic and advanced. Basic tool skills include brainstorming, cause-and-effect analysis, check sheets, data collection, graphs, histograms, multi-vari charts, and Pareto analysis. (see p. 128, *Quality Circles Tool Skills)*. Advanced tool skills used by QCs include control charts, sampling, and scattergrams.

The basic tool skills are taught to QC members during initial meetings. Six to 12 hours (meetings) are usually allowed for training in the basic tool skills and 12 to 24 hours for the advanced skills. The tool skills are at the very heart of the QC process, and it is important that QC members are well-trained in their use.

Problem-Solving Methodology

The problem-solving process (identifying, analyzing, and developing solutions to problems and implementing those solutions when feasible) is basic to QC activities. After receiving training in the problem-solving process,

QC members identify and develop a concise definition of a problem. The types of problems QC members attempt to solve range from simple house-keeping issues to complex changes in product or job designs.

The QC leader plays an important role in problem identification because if an intractable problem is selected, the group may experience frustration. Early success in solving problems helps to develop the confidence necessary for long-term QC effectiveness. Although the tools and techniques used are not complex, members unfamiliar with the structure and discipline of the QC process need time to adapt to them.

All members of the organization are invited to suggest problems for QCs to work on, but the choice of the problem must remain with the QC. This structure provides another opportunity for management to demonstrate support for the QC concept. If management selects the problems to be considered, the QC concept cannot survive.

The first step in problem solving is to identify, select, and define a problem. Then a method of measurement is selected. This enables a QC to know when the problem has been solved to the members' satisfaction. They then identify possible causes of the problem and collect data to identify the actual cause. Collecting the information required may be time-consuming and difficult. The assistance of others in the organization may be needed to obtain the necessary information. In some instances, QC members use weekly meeting time to collect information rather than meeting in a group.

Once the cause of the problem is verified, a solution is developed. At this stage, the QC members have the opportunity to apply their knowledge and experience. (The QC concept assumes that the workers are experts at their jobs.) Controls are then established to prevent recurrence of the problem, and both the solution and controls are presented to management for approval. Upon securing approval, the QC members implement their solution. This is an important part of the process because it allows them to experience "ownership" in its fullest sense. Being deprived of this experience is detrimental to their participation in the QC process. Of course, there may be instances where it is physically or legally impossible for QC members to implement the solution. In such cases, members should be allowed to maintain as much contact with the implementation process as possible by assisting the implementors (as appropriate), and the group should be provided with feedback throughout implementation. Subsequent to implementation, the approved solution is evaluated to determine its effectiveness. If successful, the solution is standardized to the extent possible and shared throughout the organization.

A final step in the process has QC members make presentations to management about the effectiveness of solutions they have implemented. There are two purposes for these presentations: to provide the QC members with recognition for their contributions and (also important) to keep management informed of the progress being made by QCs. When a QC is newly formed and recognition is most important, presentations should be made routinely. As the number of QCs increases, it becomes impractical to present the details of every solution formally to management.

Other key ingredients in the successful implementation of QCs may be called organizational prerequisites. A discussion of these requirements for success follows.

Organizational Prerequisites to Success

Organizational prerequisites are those aspects of the QC process and the environment in which it exists that must be present for success. Nine prerequisites that are either the responsibility of management or of QC members are discussed next.

Management Responsibilities

Management sets the climate in any organization, either by plan or by default. The QC process survives and thrives only in organizations where the climate for worker participation is planned and carefully managed.

Support Perhaps the primary element necessary to the success of the QC process is management support. Without continual management support, QCs may lack the necessary incentive and energy to continue. Management support (or lack of it) manifests itself in numerous ways, but can best be exemplified within the context of the steps an organization goes through in considering adoption of the QC concept. Preparatory to a decision to implement the QC process, management can demonstrate its support as follows:

- Contributing the time to listen to and understand the philosophy of QCs.
- Visiting other organizations that have implemented the QC process successfully.
- Investigating the benefits realized by other organizations that have implemented QCs successfully.
- Studying the reasons why some QC programs have failed.
- Surveying the support of all levels of management for the QC process.

Immediately subsequent to a decision to implement the QC concept, management can exhibit its support by doing the following:

- Becoming actively involved in the formation of a QC steering committee.
- Writing an implementation plan.
- Taking steps to ensure that all aspects of the implementation plan are clearly understood, especially with respect to the voluntarism concept.
- Taking the necessary precautions to ensure that common causes of failure are avoided.
- Involving unions to build a strong foundation of ownership and mutual trust.
- Taking the steps necessary to gain the support of all levels of management for the QC concept.

When the QC process is fully implemented, a number of means are available to management to reinforce its support. Among these are the following:

- Demonstrating behaviorally its commitment to the voluntarism concept.
- Providing the resources (time and funds) for training in the QC process.
- Creating a position for and employing a QC facilitator.
- Providing employees with time to conduct weekly QC meetings.
- Providing QC teams with a satisfactory meeting place and necessary supplies.
- Providing QC members with time to collect data during working hours (when feasible).
- Providing assistance to QC members when data collection (or some other task) is difficult.
- Recognizing consistently the accomplishments of QC members and leaders.
- Encouraging and attending management presentations wherein QC members make formal presentations of recommended changes.
- Providing detailed rationales to QCs when their recommendation(s) cannot be implemented.
- Attending QC meetings periodically.
- Not interfering with scheduled QC meeting times.
- Supporting the establishment of a measurement system.
- Following up to ensure that support from all levels of management is sustained.

Voluntarism Voluntary participation is an underlying principle of the QC concept. Most QC activities occur on a voluntary basis. Employees are given the freedom to choose both to join or not as the opportunity is presented and to drop out at their discretion without any fear of retribution. Sikes and associates (1980) suggest that the need for voluntary participation is not universal. Since organizational climates vary considerably, exceptions are possible, but in most instances QCs based on voluntary participation are most effective.

If employees are directed to participate in an activity like the QC process, the organization becomes vulnerable in the following ways:

- Some of the participants lack the commitment necessary to succeed.
- Such a directive is often perceived as manipulation.
- When employees have no say in the design and conduct of an activity, they do not contribute their energy and creativity to it.
- Such a management policy is likely to elicit the classic adversarial response from unions. The resulting conflict too often creates a win-lose dilemma in which both parties become entrenched in polarized positions.
- The demand that all employees participate in QC activities is inconsistent with the QC philosophy, and the resultant perceived hypocrisy is destructive throughout the organization.

For the QC process to improve productivity significantly, it is imperative that it eventually permeate every facet of the organization. When this occurs, the QC process becomes an accepted way of operating and a natural part of everyone's daily routine.

Training   Goodfellow (1981) reports that only eight of 29 companies studied experienced success in implementing a QC program. The apparent reason for the lack of success of the remainder was the failure to train the QC leaders adequately. QC facilitators, leaders, and members require training in the following skills:

- Problem-solving methodologies
- Problem-solving tools
- Statistics
- Group process issues
- Pedagogical techniques
- Management presentations

QCs are repeatedly faced with the challenge of solving problems that have eluded resolution for some time. Apart from the proper application of the problem-solving methodology and the discretionary use of appropriate QC tool skills (including statistics), problem resolution will continue to be elusive. QC participants thus need intensive training to be successful problem solvers.

In QCs, problem solving takes place in the context of group interaction. This added dynamic introduces potential group process problems. Traditionally, training in group process has been reserved for the company QC facilitators. The complexities of group process are too formidable, however, for a company QC facilitator to resolve them unassisted. When QC leaders and members are also trained in group process skills, the QC can collaborate in resolving these group process issues.

It is imperative that QC members receive training in how to deliver effective management presentations. Management presentations are one of the more important sources of recognition for QC members. Poorly organized management presentations not only thwart the members' sense of reward, they may place the entire QC process in jeopardy.

Union involvement   An adversarial relationship is likely to develop without early union representation in planning for implementation of the QC concept. Conflict emanating from such a relationship creates a win-lose situation in which the QC process is the victim. It is incumbent upon management to initiate a collaborative relationship with unions and upon union leadership to cooperate.

Patience   According to Amsden and Amsden (1980), "The most sage advice when implementing QC Circles in a company is to go slow" (p. 156). Not infrequently, management lacks the patience to limit intentionally the scope of a process it regards as promising — that is, to wait for results. It may take approximately a year for a QC to mature and experience some successes before it can attempt to solve difficult problems. If management is impatient, the QC will ultimately fail. Change is usually a slow and painstaking process.

QC Responsibilities

Cooperation is required of QC leaders and members to maintain an environment in which QCs can be effective. The organizational prerequisites to QC success that are the responsibility of QC members are discussed next.

Compliance with QC norms Quality circles function in the context of group interaction. Therefore, the behavior of group members becomes a crucial ingredient in their success. Typically, QC members mutually define behavioral norms; that is to say, they agree upon behavior that will enhance the effectiveness of the QC. If there is not compliance with QC norms, members may become disenchanted and ultimately resign.

Accountability As with individuals, the success of QCs is greatly facilitated by accountability. Goals established by QCs should be the framework for their activities. The QC that provides itself with feedback (i.e., timely information) on how performance compares to goals can modify its behavior in order to bring actual performance in line with goals. QCs must be accountable either to their own goals, their leader, the facilitator, management, or to some combination of these.

Discipline Much of the success of the QC process can be attributed to the diligent execution of the QC tool skills and the statistical principles of quality control in the context of a problem-solving methodology. There is no magic at play; perhaps there is not even a synergy. Rather, there is the self-imposed discipline of individual QC members-discipline in the faithful application of the skills they have learned. When QC members consistently and significantly depart from a disciplined approach, problem resolution diminishes, and the group becomes discouraged.

Work-related problems If a QC departs from its charter of addressing work-related problems and ventures into areas beyond its immediate sphere (e.g., compensation systems, hiring policy), its success rate may be drastically reduced and accompanying discouragement may propel it into failure. Such ventures beyond the scope of legitimate QC interests may elicit management disapproval, as well.

Patience Much the same as management, QC members must enter into the QC process with considerable patience. They must understand that problem solving is accomplished neither easily nor quickly. Failure to understand at the outset that they may not expect immediate changes in any but the smallest of problems can result in extreme frustration.

The presence of the nine prerequisites does not guarantee success nor does their absence guarantee failure. However, individually and collectively their presence will greatly enhance the probability of success. An understanding of the theoretical bases of the QC concept is another ingredient of a successful QC program. A discussion of the behavioral theory underlying the QC concept follows.

Quality Circles in Practice

Accounts of successful QC programs are currently found in weekly news magazines, trade magazines, and newspapers. Anecdotal evidence suggests that quality circles appear to have many positive effects. QCs are credited with sizable cost savings, and documented return on investments has been reported to be between two and eight to one. Reduction of product defects, increased product quality, and greater safety awareness have also been reported to have resulted from QC activities. (See p. 135, *Examples of Savings Effected Through Quality Circles Programs.*)

Nelson (1980) reports that most companies using QCs cite supervisor observations and meeting schedules as success indicators. Patchin (1981) notes that Northrop and associates cite personnel benefits, such as marked reductions in absenteeism, grievances, and terminations. Schleicher (1977) reports that attitudinal surveys reveal that a majority of participants believe that participation in a QC makes their jobs more enjoyable, improves communication with management, and improves relationships with co-workers. Almost all worker respondents believe that the programs should be expanded.

Rieker (1976) reports that the Lockheed Company developed measurement techniques to assess the effects of the QC program in its manufacturing operations. Schleicher (1977) summarizes some of the findings from this effort as follows:

- Eighty percent of the members believe that the program has had a positive effect on the quality of the work within their work team.
- Seventy percent believe that the quality of their own work has improved.
- Ninety percent believe that communications within the work team have improved as a result of the experience.
- Eighty percent believe that the cost of the program has been justified by improvements in the products turned out by their organizations.
- Twenty-five percent have given up their own time to the program.

In June 1979, the Norfolk Naval Shipyard introduced the QC process to its 12,000 employees. For every $1 invested, the QC program is estimated to have saved nearly $4 (Francis 1980). Law (1980) notes that the net savings after operating the program, including staff time and travel, was $150,000 in the first year.

Studies in both Japan and the United States have consistently claimed the following advantages of using QC programs:

- Improved communications at all levels up and down the line
- A reduction in conflicts among employees, supervisors, and management
- Improved quality
- Greater awareness of cost.

In Toyota Motor Company's quality circles and suggestion programs, over 500,000 suggestions were submitted in one year with 86 percent of them being adopted. About $2.5 million was awarded to workers for suggestions. The estimated return to the company exceeds that figure by five or six times.

Quality Circles Tool Skills

Brainstorming

Brainstorming is a method of creative thinking. The purpose of brainstorming is to facilitate unrestrained participation in the generation of ideas by all group members. Ground rules specify that any idea is acceptable. Group members share their ideas without evaluative comment from others. The rules that must be observed during the brainstorming session follow:

- **Do not criticize** anyone's ideas by word or gesture.
- **Do not discuss** any ideas during the brainstorming session, except for clarification purposes.
- **Do not hesitate** to suggest an idea, even if it sounds unrealistic. (Many times such ideas lead to a solution.)
- **Take turns.**
- **Only one idea** should be suggested at a time by each team member.
- **Do not allow negativism.**
- **Do not allow the discussion to be dominated** by one or two individuals. Everyone must get involved.
- **Do not let the brainstorming session become a gripe session.**

Brainstorming is useful during many phases of the problem-solving process, and is an invaluable tool in the QC process. In QCs, brainstorming is used for several purposes, depending on need. It is important that employees who are not QC members have an opportunity to contribute their ideas on the following:

- Problems to work on
- Possible causes of a problem
- Solutions to a problem
- Ways of implementing solutions

Cause-and-Effect Diagram

A cause-and-effect diagram is a means for collecting and organizing the possible causes of a problem. The diagram displays many "causes" but only one "effect." The effect is the problem identified during a brainstorming session; it is what needs to be corrected or changed. The causes explain the effect; that is, they are the potential reasons why the problem exists. While there may be only one or two actual causes of the problem, there are many possible causes that could appear on the cause-and-effect diagram. The construction of a cause-and-effect diagram is completed as follows:

Step 1 Draw an arrow pointing to the right:

Step 2 Place a rectangle at the point of the arrow:

Step 3 Write the effect (problem) in the rectangle (e.g., invoice errors):

Step 4 Draw diagonal lines (branches) attached to the horizontal line and attach rectangles at the ends of the diagonals:

Step 5 Inside the rectangles, write the relevant categories:

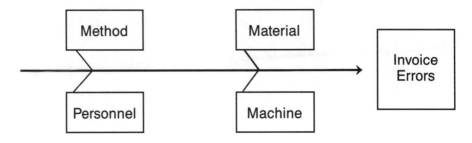

Step 6 Potential causes are identified by brainstorming. As they are identified they should be written on horizontal lines (twigs) attached to the branches. For example, when the causes of "invoice errors" are written on twigs, it might look like this:

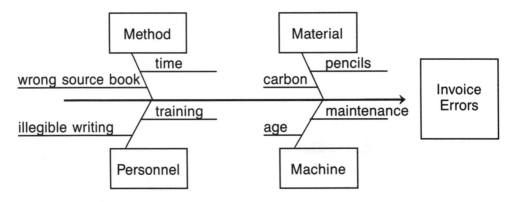

Check Sheets

Check sheets are forms for collecting information. For example, if additional information about a classroom is needed (see *Pareto Analysis* p. 133), the qualitative data collection check sheet might contain the following questions:

1. What activities take place in classroom E?
2. What type of supplies are required for those activities?
3. When, where, and how are the supplies needed in classroom E used?

Check sheets can take other forms, depending upon the information that is required. They can be used to keep track of job assignments, tasks completed, and scheduled activities in a QC, for example.

Data Collection

Data collection refers to the process of gathering information necessary to solve a problem. Check sheets (previously discussed) may be used to record the information collected.

Data may be categorized as qualitative or quantitative. In problem solving, qualitative data collection is used to identify problems (i.e., What's wrong?) and determine their extent (i.e., When and where did it happen?). Quantitative data are usually collected to determine the exact cause of a problem. During data collection activities in a QC, the group is usually divided into subgroups to ensure full participation and maximum efficiency.

During the process of solving a problem, several methods of data collection will be used. The methods usually used are: questionnaires, personal interviews, observations, experiments, and record searching.

Graph

A graph is a diagram representing successive changes over time in the value of a factor. Graphs are constructed by plotting individual measures or averages at regular checkpoints. The following graph displays faculty absences for each month.

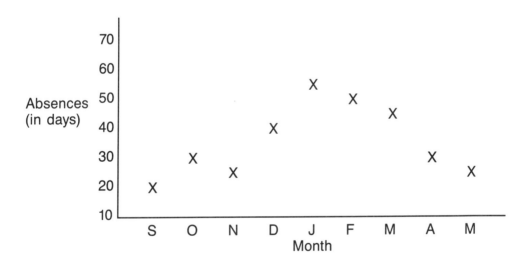

Histogram

A histogram is a graphic representation showing the pattern of data distribution. A histogram is constructed by first making a tally sheet and then replacing the tallies with rectangles proportional in height to the tallies. In the following example, the histogram illustrates the learning time in days of two classes, one using computer-aided instruction, and the other using self-programmed texts.

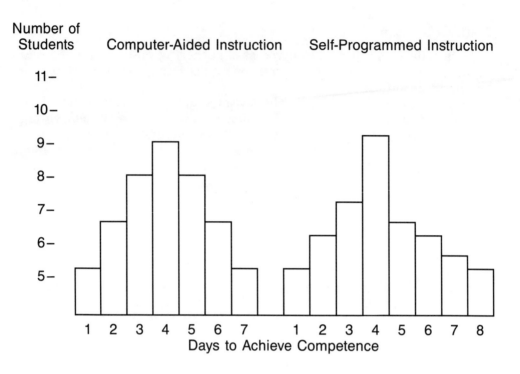

Multi-Vari Chart

A multi-vari chart is another type of graph used in data analysis. To illustrate, suppose injuries are reported at the end of each six-week period for students in automotive (A), building trades (B), and industrial (I) programs in four schools within a district. The data collected after 18 weeks are listed in the multi-vari chart that follows:

Period	School											
	1			2			3			4		
	A	B	I	A	B	I	A	B	I	A	B	I
1	3	8	10	2	6	18	2	10	8	4	2	7
2	5	7	7	7	10	6	3	7	7	6	1	12
3	2	9	7	12	15	12	1	6	10	5	1	9

The multi-vari chart that results from the data is constructed by plotting a vertical line for each program (by school) that represents the range of injuries. The multi-vari chart enables one to observe (in this case) variation by school, by program, and within the same program across the four schools.

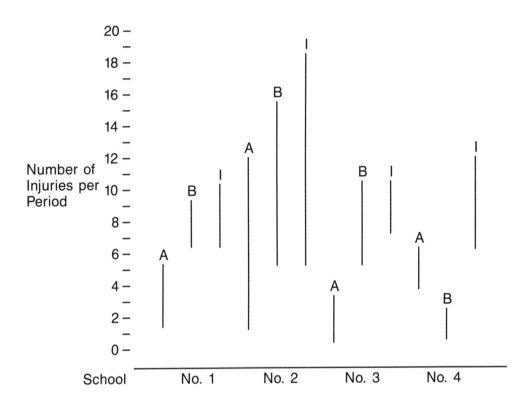

Pareto Analysis

Pareto analysis is a method of separating the most important characteristics from the least important characteristics of an event. It can be used to decide what problem to work on, to find the defect that has the highest cost, or in any other way that is useful.

Pareto analysis is a way of separating the vital factors from the trivial factors. The vital factors account for a large percentage of the effect. For example, suppose the weekly cost of supplies for eight classrooms is as follows:

Classroom	Expenditure	
E	$22.50	$32.69
B	10.19	(or 67% of the total)
C	8.16	
A	3.40	
F	1.50	
D	1.12	
H	.90	
G	.49	
Total	$48.26	

Classrooms E and B are responsible for 67 percent of the total expenditure. Classroom E and B expenditures are the *vital* factors, and the other classroom expenditures are the *trivial* factors. Usually a few factors account for a large percentage of a problem and are therefore referred to as "the vital few." The remaining factors are usually known as "the trivial many."

Pareto analysis points to the direction for further investigation. In the example just given, classrooms E and B would be investigated to find out why their costs account for such a large percentage of the total cost of supplies. To make the vital factors readily apparent, the results might be displayed graphically.

Examples of Savings Effected Through Quality Circles Programs

The examples presented in this appendix are based on experiences of both blue-collar and white-collar workers. Some of the examples involve operations that are common to both education and industry.

- An estimated $636,000 was saved by the purchasing department at Westinghouse Electronics Systems Center in Baltimore by initiating a new procedure wherein overshipments by vendors are returned to them at their own expense. This procedure was suggested by a QC committee (Nelson 1980).

- At Honeywell, in St. Petersburg, Florida, where approximately 130 QCs are active, savings were documented in actual product cost reductions of over $500,000 — a six-to-one return on investment (Nelson 1980).

- The General Electric Company's room-air-conditioner plant in Columbia, Tennessee, achieved a $15,000 annual savings by solving a weld-leak problem (Nelson 1980).

- A QC at Northrop solved the problem of continual breakage of bits used to drill holes in titanium for airplanes. By changing the drilling angle and using bits made of harder steel, the QCs ended estimated losses of $28,000 in lost time (Gottschalk 1980).

- Management of a General Motors plant in Tarrytown, New York, was considering closing the plant down because of high absenteeism and poor product quality. The number of outstanding employee grievances against management totaled 2,000. Since QCs began to hold meetings to discuss complaints and ideas for boosting efficiency, the number of outstanding grievances has dropped to 30, and absenteeism has been reduced to 2.5 percent ("Stunning Turnaround at Tarrytown" 1980).

- At the Lockheed Company, a QC made up of machinists determined that the installation of travel-dial indicators on four machine tools would improve the quality of their products. The indicators not only improved product quality, but also increased machine efficiency by 20 percent. This resulted in better quality products at a savings of $3,000 per year. (Taken from an internal unpublished report at Lockheed Missile and Space Company, Inc., Sunnyvale, California, "Lockheed QC Circle," 1976, p. 4.)

- At the Continental Bank in Chicago, annual cash savings ranging from $1,700 to $30,000 have resulted from only eight months of QC activities. The problems addressed included phone procedures for customer inquiries and complaints, more effective use of automated systems, and faster servicing of personal banking (Aubrey and Fencel 1982).

- At Sherwin-Williams in Richmond, Kentucky, productivity increased by 30 percent, unit cost of paint decreased by 45 percent, failure costs were reduced by 25 percent, and the percentage of goods returned was down by 75 percent. These benefits were achieved through utilizing the plant's human resources in QCs (Posa 1981).

- At the Lockheed Company, a QC developed a method to mold a plastic part assembly in two instead of five steps. The redesigned assembly is lighter and stronger than its predecessor, and has resulted in an estimated savings of $160,000 over the life of the contract. Since 1974, Lockheed's savings from its QC program are estimated at almost $3 million, six times the cost of operating the program (Reiker 1976).

Suggestion Systems*

This section was written by the author while he was Manager, Quality Initiatives, Defense Systems Division, at Honeywell Inc. This section reflects Honeywell's highly successful program as well as data on a number of other suggestion systems.

A suggestion system is a structured and understood process that allows all employees to submit ideas to better their environment, work efficiency, or product quality. The system must assure fair and timely evaluation of the ideas. It must also at least provide recognition for ideas used and usually some form of reward as well.

Purposes and Objectives

The purpose of a suggestion system should be communication. First, it must assure that all ideas of *all* employees will be fairly considered. Second, it must assure the satisfaction and *self-esteem* generated by having one's ideas used. Third, it should offer a variety of forms of recognition and rewards, both for the suggesters and for those performing the evaluations. Fourth, it must provide fair answers within a reasonable time. These lead to satisfaction and recognition for the originator of the idea and also provide role model leadership for others.

The objective of a suggestion system is to allow all employees to use their minds; to work smarter, not just harder; and to participate in the basics of industrial democracy, where all have a voice.

Objections to Suggestion Systems

Many companies have tried suggestion systems and dropped them. Many maintain systems that are little-used. Many have a decidedly negative attitude toward them. Such objections are usually based on one of two premises:

- We are not going to pay out money for ideas that people should share voluntarily.
- The costs of running these programs far exceed the real dollars saved.

The following comments can be made on these two premises:

- Paying out money for ideas is a basic American concept. The suggestion system pays for ideas *beyond* the job scope and beyond what we are paying regular salaries for. We need the very best ideas. It is only fair to compensate for them.

---

*Reprinted with permission from "Suggestion Systems," by Robert A. Schwarz. *Human Resources Management and Development Handbook,* edited by William R. Tracey, Ed. D. Copyright 1985 by AMACOM, American Management Association.

- Suggestion systems may or may not appear to be profitable, depending
  on how the savings and cost data are collected. Most systems will exceed
  a breakeven if honestly measured. These systems also contribute to a
  favorable work attitude, which has a major — but not strictly measurable
  — impact on worker efficiency.

The American Culture

America is a nation of individuals reared to value the Horatio Alger ideal.
As a nation, we are different from Japan, where much of the economic
initiative is currently based. Bill Ouchi, in his "Theory Z" videotape,
compares the group culture of rice planting in Japan to the single-family
farms in the United States. In growing rice, a group of families working
together grow far more product than if they worked individually. Our culture
is based on the "family farm"-type individual and has revered the Einstein,
Edison, and Henry Ford types for their *individual accomplishments*. A
suggestion system is a singular method for putting the individualistic and
capitalistic orientation of our nation to work for the industrial communication process. A suggestion system reinforces and rewards the creative person
who puts forth the effort to research and present ideas.

In our culture we have a variety of types of persons. Some are quiet and
shy and would rarely assume that their ideas are worth presenting. Others,
less shy, are group-oriented and do not seek individual visibility. These types
may truly blossom as sources for ideas under the quality circles technique.
Others may rarely be involved in creative thought. They may, however,
respond to group incentives, where goals for a department or a whole
company focus on a series of concerns.

Regarding motivation and creativity, one consideration that arises from
our culture is the size of the group with which we are working. This consideration can be summarized as follows:

- One person, creative and desiring recognition: A suggestion system
  provides the needed mechanism.
- Ten to 20 persons, creative and group-oriented: A quality circles or
  similar "circle" process uses synergism to generate ideas.
- Fifty or more persons with common problems: Group goals are required
  to provide focus for action.

Essential Conditions for Suggestion Systems

Any employee communication process (suggestion system, quality circles,
and so on) is a form of industrial democracy, which means that a new
relationship between labor and management is being established. This
requires certain conditions if success is to be achieved.

Top management's enthusiastic support, commitment, and involvement.
The changes involved in developing and implementing a suggestion system
are not something to be assigned to a middle-level manager. These changes

are a basic alteration to a "family" structure and require a lot of support throughout the organization. Table 1 shows a statistical comparison between average suggestion system performance in a cross section industrial group and suggestion system performance at the Honeywell Defense Systems Division. The data illustrate widespread acceptance of the suggestion system process among eligible (factory) employees — as measured by the high number of suggestions received per employee — coupled with strong management support in encouraging rapid processing of each suggestion by the engineers.

Middle-management involvement. Much training and understanding among middle management is needed to generate ownership of any suggestion system process being proposed. If true ownership is not generated, the program will be perceived merely as more work, not as a priority target (like profit). And that kind of program will be regarded as a no-win proposition.

Table 1. Suggestion System Performance: Statistical Comparison Between 1980 Industrial Group Average Data and 1981 Honeywell Defense Systems Division Data

	1980 Industry Group Composite	*1981 Honeywell Defense Systems Division*
Suggestions received per eligible employee per year	.12	2.47
Percentage of suggestions received that were adopted	26	48
Average processing time	130 days	62 days (Dec. 1981 data)

(SOURCE: National Association of Suggestion Systems, 230 North Michigan Avenue, Suite 1200, Chicago, Illinois 60601. Used by permission.)

An experienced program leader. It is critical that any employee communication process be staffed with prime management. Installing a suggestion system requires an experienced manager who understands politics and has enough personal clout to ensure success. This is not an assignment for the "new employee," to enable him or her to get a good look at all departments. It is likewise inappropriate for an employee nearing retirement, where the opportunity for long-term planning is lost.

Acceptance by the rank and file. A new suggestion system will be met with a variety of employee attitudes. These will reflect the basic company environment. The suggestion system concept is usually favorably received, but a lot of attention will be paid to how fairly and promptly the ideas are handled. Some observations:

1. Change is always welcomed (Hawthorne effect).
2. Recognition of intellectual self-worth is positive.
3. The premise that ideas beget profits will make for suspicion if not properly handled.

Starting the program at an appropriate time. Never start when the program is expected to solve a worker/management problem, *or* when union negotiations are in need of a favorable "bone." *Start* when there is an opportunity to focus thinking on the new suggestion system — *not* when other changes are being initiated that compete for visibility. *Start* when supporting engineering or evaluation groups can be free from budget cycles, inventories, or other time-consuming cyclic activities.

Putting the perceived $$$$$$ into perspective. Invariably the person submitting an idea is proud of it and considers it to be of significant worth to the company. But frequently the person evaluating dozens of ideas (some good, many poor) feels that more time is spent (wasted) than the ideas yield in value. The realities need to be communicated to both groups. The value of ideas (even the less-than-earthshaking ones) must not be put down. The suggestion system must communicate the message that through the suggestion process emerge advances or improvements in profit that can help build jobs and futures by enhancing competitive positioning.

Starting a Suggestion System

The success of a suggestion system hinges on a number of factors, ranging from management support to staffing to tracking and reporting suggestions. The following paragraphs discuss many of the most important ones.

Management Support

The support of a qualified consultant or field trips to companies with working suggestion systems, or both, are necessary first steps. Be sure that the top executive involved in the implementation is also involved in deciding on the start-up. Try to involve as many executives/managers as possible in the decision-making process. Establish a committee that represents all involved levels and departments to generate policies. Members of this committee will then guide progress and establish acceptance and ownership in their own areas. Figure 1 illustrates a procedure for processing suggestions similar to what might be developed by such a committee. It is a reduction of a 17-inch by 22-inch four-color poster, with the colors on the poster matching the colors on the four-part suggestion form.

Once a determination to proceed is made, the next step is to staff the project.

Staffing and Organization

A good suggestion system manager/administrator needs an understanding of the working environment and the acceptance of upper management. This defines a senior, qualified middle manager. The impact of the suggestion system process is powerful, and it must be guided carefully on a day-to-day basis. The manager will require clerical and administrative support in proportion to the size of the job.

Organization reporting relationships vary. Many programs report to the personnel department. Some report to industrial engineering or production. Honeywell's reports to quality. There is no set rule. The program must be placed where it can be most effective.

Funding

The next decision is how to fund the suggestion system process. There are two options to consider. First, the program costs could be paid from a central fund, usually charged back as a burden prorate. This would include cash awards, staff costs, PR expenses, and so on. The second option is to charge direct cash awards to the burden of the department that employs the person submitting the suggestion. In the majority of cases, the idea benefits the department, and the increased burden is offset by efficiency. Charges for the suggestion system staff, PR activities, and similar costs would be allocated as a burden prorate across the whole organization.

Arguments can be made against both funding approaches. These include:

• The departments may delay suggestions due to the costs that would be charged back to them.
• The departments may not effectively filter "junk ideas," since the cost result is not charged to them.

Either way, a budget must be set up and accountability established.

Legal Considerations

There are basic legal rights and relationships associated with a suggestion system. The system becomes in fact a contract between the management of the company and all employees. It is important to clearly state the rules on:

• Who decides on awards and their value.
• What appeals procedure exists.
• Who owns the ideas submitted.

There is an excellent professional group, National Association of Suggestion Systems (NASS), that can provide extensive help in these (and other) areas. It has made a detailed study of the legal considerations that warrant review by company counsel before forms and rule books are designed.

Cash Awards, Drawings, Pats on the Back

The programs in effect at many companies include a wide variety of award plans:

- One company pays 15 percent of the first two years' savings, with a maximum award of $50,000.
- Another company provides nominal gift awards — no cash. (Both companies are near the top of the Fortune 500 list.)

Figure 1. ECR (Error Cause Removal) Road to Results Poster Shows How
Each Suggestion Is Processed

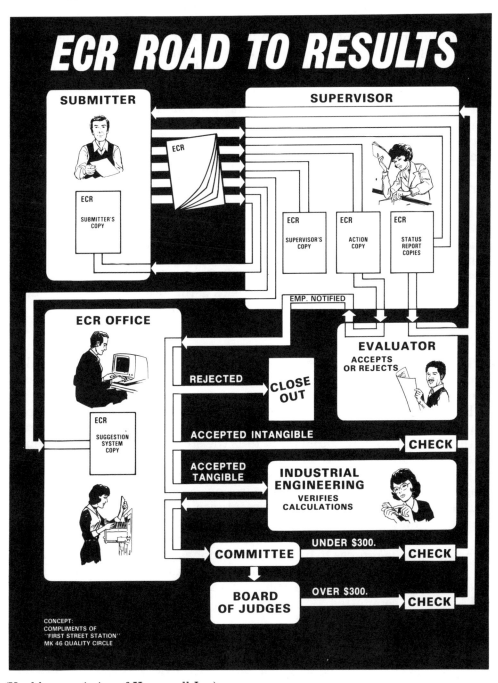

(Used by permission of Honeywell Inc.)

- Still another large company makes nominal awards for each implemented idea and conducts drawings for travel prizes. In most cases, there
is no relationship between the amount of the savings and the size of
the award.
- The program at Honeywell, Minneapolis Operations, provides one sixth
of the first year's gross savings, with a maximum award of $5,000 per
suggestion. There is no limit on the number of awards per individual.

However, people generally want to know what they will get for their effort.
Therefore, a ratio of savings such as that used at Honeywell is best. Also,
the award maximum should not be set too high, because a large award may
encourage collusion, such as doctoring manufacturing processes for future
changes or kickbacks between engineers and eligible employees.

Forms

The foregoing five steps are essential preliminaries to designing forms.
The first decision is to determine whether submitters will be anonymous
or identified on the form. There are arguments both ways. Honeywell chooses
to have the submitter's name visible. Others feel some discrimination could
result if personalities became involved. Figure 2 shows the front of a
Honeywell suggestion system form; the back of the form contains a summary
of the program rules to conform to a legal requirement.

Training/Education

The Honeywell program has been in effect for years, but there is still a
need to educate. Old employees tend to forget, and turnover provides a
continuing crop of new workers.

Bulletin boards are used extensively in the education process, as are a
variety of articles in the house newspapers. A good 35 mm slide program
with an accompanying sound track tells the story in nine minutes. Memos
and notices are also used as appropriate.

Initiating a new program requires the understanding that many professional "trainees" will regard a suggestion system as a lot of work. The
training must be tailored to gain acceptance for the system in your environment. This is where top-management involvement really comes in. When
the director of a department makes a presentation on the suggestion system's
benefits and the process to be used, and emphasizes personal commitment
to the system, dedication throughout the operation results. If personal
presentations are not feasible, consider a videotaped message. Make sure
all levels are committed.

First Suggestions

The first suggestions into the system are critical. They not only test the
process but they must also prove the integrity of the system to suggesters.
Be sure to be honest about these first efforts. If they are unusable or just

"cute," suggesters need a mature communication. Supervisors will need help in handling some situations. Evaluators will need advice on how to turn down an idea without turning off the source (kind words don't always come easily). Also, make sure the response time by each group handling the suggestions can be measured. If delays occur, find out where the ideas are being held up and fix the process.

And finally, publicize the positive results. Make everyone aware of some of the good ideas. Use posters, presentations, videotapes, newsletters, and so on to build the image of successful suggesters. Make it fun to be a winner. Figures 3 and 4 show typical posters that can be used to publicize the benefits of collaboration and spread the news of success.

Tracking and Reporting the Suggestion Data

To track each suggestion, at least the following data are needed:

1. Date submitted
2. Department of submitter
3. Department assigned to review
4. Disposition
5. Awards/savings
6. Completion date

Depending on the size of the program, this information can be tracked manually or by computer. It doesn't take much to make a computerized suggestion system cost-effective.

Reports should be set up so that some positive thinking can be done, such as:

- Recognizing departments with the largest ratio of suggesters or dollars saved.
- Recognizing individuals who have a high participation rate, on the basis of awards earned or number of ideas submitted.
- Recognizing evaluators who have a good record of answering suggestions promptly.

The report structure is the key to using the data in a way that will really keep the program moving.

Figure 2. Suggestion System Form Used by Honeywell

(Used by permission of Honeywell Inc.)

Figure 3. Poster Showing How a Bright Idea Leads to an ECR (Error Cause Removal) Suggestion

(Used by permission of Honeywell Inc.)

Figure 4. A 17-inch by 22-inch Poster Printed to Promote Honeywell's 1978 Suggestion Program

(Used by permission of Honeywell Inc.)

Recognition

Honeywell holds a lot of recognition activities. The value of having such an ongoing program for recognizing outstanding participants in the suggestion system has been proved through comparison of historic data from before and after changes have been made in recognition processes. There is significant evidence that high recognition yields a much greater number of productive ideas.

Honeywell's recognition approaches include:

- Using top management to present awards. High-level executives can be used for maximum awards, middle management for smaller awards, and so on. Also, take pictures; publicize.
- Displaying posters featuring high-award winners. These serve to recognize the person as well as share the suggested ideas throughout the company.
- Selecting an annual "top suggester." This person, along with others identified by fellow members of the National Association of Suggestion Systems, is presented a special award by the governor of Minnesota.
- Publishing articles in the company newspaper on high-award winners.
- Presenting gift awards to persons achieving high levels of savings. Suggesters earning $500 or more in awards are invited to a special recognition luncheon. Invitations to the luncheon can also be given to supervisors whose departments have achieved high annual savings through suggestions.
- Holding special award programs for selected evaluators who are doing a top job.
- Inviting supervisors whose employees' suggestions produced high annual savings to a recognition luncheon.
- Presenting participants with plaques, certificates, pens, mugs, matches, and coasters. All such award items are useful as a means of making the program highly visible to potential suggesters.

Reviewing the Suggestion System

Honeywell has a board of judges composed of management representatives of each area involved in the suggestion system. The board's task is to determine policy, evaluate high-award suggestions, and respond to complaints or problems. A strong board is needed to take pressure off the program's administrator/manager. Board members can be rotated, with a two- to five-year assignment typical. A board meets no more than once a month.

Reporting to Management

The suggestion system should include a monthly report to keep management informed of the program's accomplishments and problems. Key areas of concern, such as maintaining a rapid turnaround for responding to suggestions, should be highlighted.

Suggestion Systems and Quality Circles

"Circle"-type programs can complement suggestion systems. Adding quality circles to the existing suggestion system at Honeywell resulted in an increase in individual suggestions stimulated by "circle" activity. The suggestion system originally offered payout to either an individual or a team. The concept of team was extended to include all the nonexempt persons in the quality circle. The procedure is to take the total award and divide it by the number of nonexempt circle members. Rules provide a $10 award for exempt suggesters. This way, all circle members get an award; however, there can be wide differences between exempt employees getting a $10 award and nonexempt employees sharing awards of up to $5,000.

Another approach is to divide the award by the total number of circle members and pay that amount to the nonexempt members only. One major circle user does not pay any awards to circles for ideas, believing that recognition is appropriate for circles and cash awards for individuals.

It is interesting to note that the start of quality circles at Honeywell over four years ago stimulated an increase in suggestion submissions. However, the circles account for less than 1 percent of the suggestions. This reinforces the belief that both circles and a suggestion system are needed to reach different cultures and accommodate different needs.

Summary

A suggestion system is a basic element — if not the basic element — for communication in most U.S. organizations. It meets the need for individual recognition and individual creativity. A suggestion system supports other techniques (circles, incentives, and so on). But while circles, incentives, and other programs are usually intermittent, a suggestion system provides a continuous, fundamental avenue of communication.

Honeywell's suggestion system policies and procedures follow. They will give the reader a more detailed look at the major considerations involved in setting up and running such a program.

Suggestion System Policies and Procedures for Cash Awards

Foreword

This procedure outlines the current policy and procedure of the Suggestion System. It has been developed and approved by members of the Board of Judges to maintain consistent application of the Suggestion System. The information is considered Company Property, and you are asked to return your copy to the Administrator of the Suggestion System when you are not directly involved in the operation of the Suggestion System.

1.0 Scope

This procedure covers the objectives of the Suggestion System, the duties and responsibilities of personnel in administering the system, and rules and procedures for implementing the system.

2.0 Objectives

Objectives of the Suggestion System are to provide:

- An organized method for all eligible employees to submit constructive ideas on matters which are beyond the normal expectancy of their duties or responsibilities.
- An investigation that is unbiased, consistent, prompt, and efficient.
- Benefits for employees whose Suggestions are adopted and constructive, tactful rejection of unacceptable ideas accompanied by the reason for rejection.
- A follow-up which ensures that all personnel involved directly or indirectly with the Suggestion System are performing their functions properly and that all benefits from this system are being realized.
- A Suggestion System which assists in improving the economic status of the Company.

3.0 Organization

3.1 Board of Judges

A Board of Judges governs the Suggestion System.

3.1.1 Membership. The Board of Judges consists of five to seven members. These members are representatives obtained on a rotating basis from all departments.

3.1.2 Responsibilities. Responsibilities of the Board of Judges are to:

- Provide an organized method by which employees can submit constructive ideas for managerial analysis and, if the ideas are accepted, receive monetary awards.

- Provide a method of evaluating employee Suggestions which is unbiased, consistent, prompt, and efficient.
- Interpret and clarify Suggestion rules and eligibility requirements.
- Propose changes and amend rules, with appropriate Management approval, to increase the effectiveness of the employee Suggestion System.
- Review Subcommittee recommendations for all awards over $300 and take final action.
- Assume final authority on its decisions relative to the awards to be paid by the Suggestion System, including the denial of any award or eligibility for an award.
- Establish Subcommittees as required and appoint Subcommittee members.
- Delegate duties and responsibilities to the Subcommittees in such a way as to establish and maintain a fully effective Suggestion System.

3.2 Subcommittees

3.2.1 Membership. Subcommittees are all made up of qualified people obtained on a rotating basis from departments, and they are appointed and maintained by the Board of Judges. No more than one new member is to be appointed to a Subcommittee in any three-month period. Subcommittee Chairpersons are appointed by the Board of Judges.

3.2.2 Types of Subcommittees. Subcommittees could be:

- The Office Subcommittee, which deals with Suggestions from nonexempt Office and Technical employees.
- The Factory Subcommittee, which deals with Suggestions from hourly paid Factory personnel.
- The Toolroom/Maintenance Subcommittee, which deals with Suggestions from those areas.

3.2.3 Responsibilities. The responsibilities of Subcommittee members are to:

- Maintain a consistent policy in applying the Suggestion System rules in the Factory, Office, and other areas as assigned by the Board of Judges.
- Review all approved ideas.
- Determine final disposition of any idea entailing an award of $300 or less.
- Act as arbitrator in any dispute between personnel as to the validity or feasibility of a Suggestion.
- Request, if required, the actual personnel involved in a dispute to appear before the Subcommittee until a decision is reached.
- Aid in establishing rules of operation.
- Act, at the request of the Subcommittee Chairperson, as special investigators or in assisting concerned supervisors to evaluate ideas.

3.3 Administrator

The responsibilities of the Administrator of the Suggestion System are to:

- Maintain a Suggestion System Procedure Manual, which contains guidelines for consistent interpretation of policy and rules in the Factory and Office areas. Any changes to this manual must be approved by the Board of Judges.
- Coordinate the administration of the system with the Investigators, the Subcommittee, and the Board of Judges.
- Maintain the records necessary for efficient functioning of the system.
- Coordinate the investigation of Suggestions in such a way that a fair and logical conclusion can be reached on each idea.
- Analyze the backlog of Suggestions.
- Prepare reports of the effectiveness of the Suggestion System to management.
- Act as employee representative at the meeting held by the Board of Judges.
- Aid in review of all appealed Suggestions.
- Prepare data for Board/Subcommittee review.

4.0 Rules of Eligibility

4.1 General

To be eligible for cash award, a Suggestion must be submitted by an eligible employee or eligible employee group on an eligible subject beyond the normal expectancy of the suggester's duties or responsibilities; and it must recommend an action which, when adopted, will result in a saving or improvement to the Company. Employees will not receive awards for carrying out their work assignments.

Employees in the trades (electricians, machinists, plumbers, carpenters, general maintenance, tool makers, tool designers, technicians, etc.) are employed specifically to utilize the arts and skills of their craft and to apply them to maintenance and repairs of buildings, machinery, and equipment. They are expected to use their knowledge and experience to avoid recurrence of a breakdown or a condition calling for their assignment to this specific job or area.

If the Suggestion is outside the job scope or the work assignment, the Suggestion is eligible for award.

4.2 Eligible Employees

All factory nonexempt employees, including part-time employees, and nonexempt administrative personnel are eligible, with the exception of the Suggestion System Administrator. The Company controls the right to determine the classification of the exempt/nonexempt employees.

4.3 Eligible Subjects

4.3.1 Types of Subjects. Subjects which are eligible for Suggestions include those that would result in:

- Savings in time, material, scrap, rework, or tooling.
- Improvements in products, safety, or working conditions.
- Elimination or reduction of layout or paperwork errors where cost savings are involved.
- Improvements in systems or in procedures which are performed in regular established systems for record or cost purposes.

4.3.2 Limitations on Eligible Subjects. Some limitations, primarily of time, are involved in submission of Suggestions on eligible subjects. These include the following:

- Subjects must pertain to equipment or methods formalized by layouts or written operating procedures. Informal methods or oral instructions are not valid subjects for Suggestions.
- All products manufactured or methods used by the factory will be eligible for Suggestion 90 days after layouts, inspection procedures, prints, and/or designs are originally issued. New tooling, equipment, and machines installed on the production floor and ready to run production parts will be eligible for a cash award 90 days after qualification and/or production acceptance. There are no time limitations on safety ideas. Eligibility prior to this date would be at the discretion of the Manager. This would be formalized by a memo from the Manager to the Board of Judges.
- Ideas for salvaging parts are not eligible for a period of two weeks from the date the parts are rejected.
- The Suggestion must be submitted within 15 days of the time it was mentioned or first used in the department.

4.4 Ineligible Subjects and/or Proposals

Subjects which are ineligible for cash awards include those which:

- Pertain to routine maintenance such as repairing worn tools or equipment, installing, moving, or cleaning lights, plumbing, paint work, etc.
- Deal with Company policy or managerial decisions such as negotiated labor contracts, employee benefits, public relations, recreation, parking program, etc. It is a matter of Company policy or managerial decision to decide if and when jobs are to be run in the plant or subcontracted; therefore, sourcing ideas are ineligible and not open to Suggestions.
- Concern motivational programs, publicity, or slogans.
- Pertain to proposals already under active consideration by the Company.
- Apply to inspection procedure revisions dealing with sampling plans.
- Concern feeds and speeds.

4.5 Time Suggestion Is Valid

A suggester's idea is protected, if properly submitted, until such time as award is made or suggester is notified that the idea is not acceptable. If a Suggestion is not approved when submitted but is put into effect within two years from the date of rejection, the employee has the right to bring his original Suggestion up for award. All Suggestions shall remain active for two years from date of decision. Such suggestions may be resubmitted before expiration of the two-year period if the idea still seems to be of value or has been implemented.

5.0 Investigation of Ideas

The Investigator and Implementing Supervisor must carefully and impartially evaluate each idea, taking into account all savings factors.

5.1 Types of Ideas

In general, Suggestion ideas fall into the following categories:

Cost reductions — e.g., savings in labor, materials, machine hours, downtime. Some questions to ask here are, does it:

- Substitute machine operation for hand operation?
- Reduce personnel-hours for operation?
- Reduce or eliminate materials use?
- Save energy?
- Reduce workload for rental machines?
- Substitute less costly materials?
- Reduce waste?
- Increase output per machine?
- Prevent breakage or prolong life of tools, equipment, or machinery?
- Improve design or function of equipment?
- Change tools or equipment to reduce manufacturing time?
- Change flow of materials to eliminate unneeded operations?
- Combine forms?
- Combine operations to reduce costs?
- Improve handling and storage?
- Save paper or other supplies?

Product improvement — i.e., any idea which betters the quality, performance, appearance, construction, or utility of our product. Questions include:

Are defects reduced or eliminated?
- Is eye appeal improved?
- Is product more dependable?
- Will performance of device be improved?

Safety — i.e., ways to reduce accidents or fire hazards. These ideas may involve:

- Calling attention to unsafe practices.
- Recommending installation of guards.
- Use of protective clothing or equipment not normally available.
- Fire prevention measures.

Convenience — i.e., changes which make a job easier or more pleasant, although there are generally no tangible savings involved, and which would have a direct effect on improving employee morale.

5.2 Recording Information

Investigation information is recorded on the ACTION COPY in "Disposition" block on front of form, on the reverse side of the ACTION COPY, or on a suitable attachment to the ACTION COPY. The report is completed by the Investigator with sign-off by both the Implementing Supervisor and the originator's Supervisor. In those cases where there may be some doubt as to whether or not the submitter's suggestion is within or outside of his job scope or responsibility, the immediate Supervisor must make a preliminary decision and obtain concurrence and sign-off by the next level of supervision.

5.3 Investigators

An employee's immediate Supervisor is responsible for investigation of the Suggestions. Responsibilities include:

- Investigation of Suggestions and/or coordinating the investigation with other personnel who can best evaluate the specific idea.
- Assurance that investigations are fair and impartial.

5.4 Sequence of Investigation

The following sequence should be followed in investigating an idea submitted as a Suggestion:

- Read and analyze idea.
- Recommend disposition (accepted or unapproved).
- Approve or obtain approval of Implementing Supervisor.
- Evaluate savings factors of accepted ideas and submit to Industrial Engineering for verification.
- Submit to Suggestion Office.

5.5 Investigation Procedures

The following are the major procedures that should be observed in investigating and evaluating Suggestions.
In reading and analyzing an idea:

- Check the basic schedule and estimate the value of the idea to determine how much time should be spent on the investigation.
- Estimate dollar expenditures required to put idea into effect.
- Approve idea or contact Implementing Supervisor to discuss its merits

with him or her — i.e., the economics of installation and the savings possibilities.

Practical ideas should be put into effect as soon as possible:

- Contact the necessary people for action.
- Explore related applications.
- Notify suggester if use of the idea is to be delayed 30 days or more.
- Establish a tickler file to remind investigators to follow up action.

Evaluate cost savings. An acceptable Suggestion must result in a cost saving or be of positive value to the Company. Implementation cost is not deducted in arriving at the annual savings for award calculations. All implementation costs should be recovered within one year (capital equipment is an exception to this rule), or the idea is not economically justified. Calculate the hours saved by comparing the new method to the old using approved rates. Estimates will be required when approved rates are not available.

Determine the gross savings for one year. Evaluate all savings factors. Find hours saved by comparing new method to old using time for a normal operator at 100 percent performance in both instances. The labor rates (do not include burden) to be used for savings calculations are obtained from the Suggestion Administrator.

Evaluate material saved — e.g., quantity reduction in paper usage or cost reduction by use of cheaper form or brand of merchandise.

Evaluate reduction of rental equipment costs. Find hours saved by comparing new method to old. Actual rental rates are used in arriving at the dollar figure.

Record date idea went into effect.

If suggestion is unacceptable, give logical reason why.

If idea is accepted, provide a brief summary of it to facilitate Committee and Board member review. To prevent misunderstanding, the investigator should restate in his or her own words on the evaluation sheet the suggested ideas, and the disposition write-ups should contain a direct statement on why the suggester's idea is accepted.

If results of putting an acceptable idea into effect fall into the "intangible" category — i.e., the exact cost of the two methods cannot be determined or the savings are not easily measured or possible to measure — give award recommendation and reason for it. *Do not use the intangible award* if the results of the suggested change can be measured. An intangible award will be considered accomplished and installed when the change has been initiated through revised documentation or initiated procedure.

Provide information needed for Subcommittee and Board of Judges review, including:

- Certification that idea is in use and the effective date of installation.

- Comparison of old and new methods, listing all savings factors. If intangible, give award recommendation.
- If idea is unacceptable for use, give logical reason why. Suggester must be made to feel the idea has been carefully considered and any merits realized.

6.0 Awards

6.1 Basic Award

The basic award subject to the maximum set out in Section 6.2 is one sixth of the *gross* savings realized from the first year's application of an accepted idea. The gross award may range from $5 up to a maximum of $5,000. Awards are considered as salary and are subject to withholding.

6.2 Maximum Award

The maximum award which will be awarded by the Board of Judges for any application of a Suggestion is $5,000. Unless savings to justify the full award have already been realized, an initial award of $2,000 is paid upon acceptance of the Suggestion, and the balance is paid on recalculation after the idea has been in use one full year. There is no interest paid on the "deferred balance."

6.3 Minimum Award

The minimum award is $5 per Suggestion and is authorized for any application of a Suggestion in which the calculated award would be $5 or less. Do not use the word *minimum* award in recommendation.

6.4 Intangible Award

An intangible award is recommended when savings cannot be calculated. It is either a $5 award for documentation corrections or ideas of convenience that tend to improve working conditions and/or employee morale or a $20 award for ideas where savings logic exists but the savings are difficult to quantify.

6.5 Safety Award

A $20 safety award is recommended for accepted safety suggestions.

6.6 Split Award/Joint Contributors/Team Suggestion/Quality Circles

A split award is the division of an award among two or more employees who submit an accepted Suggestion jointly or individually on the same date. The amount is calculated as a single award and divided equally among the eligible recipients. In the case of a Team Suggestion, the award is shared equally by eligible, nonexempt Team members involved in the submission. Exempt Team members will be given a $10 recognition award. "Team" awards are limited to safety and tangible awards only.

6.7 Action Award

An action award is made when the Suggestion motivates the solution of a problem which is not the solution proposed by the suggester. An action award is valued at 50 percent of the basic award, or $\frac{1}{12}$ of the first year's savings from the improved idea.

When the suggester's idea could have saved $600 (resulting in an award of $100), but a different solution is used saving $900, on which an action award would be $75, the suggester is entitled to the greater sum.

As a rule of thumb:

- A *full award* is paid when the employee Suggestion is workable, although it may be modified or improved by Engineering to increase savings.
- An *action award* is paid when the original employee Suggestion is not workable, but Engineering, as an outgrowth of the Suggestion at the time of the investigation, develops a *drastically different solution* to solve the same problem.

6.8 Reapplication Ideas

Reapplication ideas — i.e., new and specific applications of an existing method — are paid the full award (one sixth of a year's savings).

6.9 Buying a Principle

In "buying a principle," the award is for results that are part tangible and part intangible and is in full payment for all *known* or *anticipated* future applications of the principle. If, however, after the idea has been communicated to its areas of use and they have had the opportunity to put it in use (15 to 90 days), the suggester calls attention to an unforeseen or overlooked application possibility, he is eligible for an award based on that specific application.

6.10 Duplicate Ideas

If a Suggestion which duplicates an earlier, rejected one actually brings about corrective action, a full award is paid to the original suggester (provided it is within the two-year time limit), and an action award (50 percent) goes to the second suggester.

6.11 Former Employees and Retirees

If an employee should leave the Company before an award is approved, payment is still made upon approval of an idea in the same manner as if the suggester were still an employee.

7.0 Reasons for Nonacceptance

An employee who submits a Suggestion is entitled to a full and logical explanation of why an idea is not acceptable. As a guide to evaluating an idea and providing an explanation of nonacceptance, the following paragraphs list a number of reasons why a Suggestion might be rejected:

- The idea is not economically feasible under present conditions — e.g., schedule limitations, excessive cost of installation, space problems.
- A duplicate prior Suggestion is under active consideration.
- The idea is currently being implemented or evaluated.
- The idea is vague or incomplete, requires further explanation.
- The subject matter is ineligible — e.g., contrary to Company policy or customer or government requirements.
- The subject matter falls within the scope of the suggester's job assignment. An employee under direct assignment to correct a problem is not eligible for an award for suggesting a solution to that problem.
- The idea does not solve the problem posed, or the problem does not exist.
- The Suggestion creates a new problem.
- The idea does not eliminate a hazard.
- The submittal is a complaint — not a Suggestion.
- The procedure suggested is considered general "shop practice."
- The Suggestion corrects an obvious typographical error on some form of documentation.
- The Suggestion involves routine maintenance-general repair, painting, heating, worn tools, illegible paperwork, etc.
- The Suggestion concerns jobs set up on a temporary basis.

8.0 Company Rights

Company rights involved in the Suggestion System are:

- The Company reserves the right at any time without notice to terminate, amend, or extend the Suggestion System.
- The Company assumes no legal responsibility beyond the maximum award for any suggestion.
- The employee assigns all rights to the Company, including patents.
- The employee has the right to appeal, but the reviewed action of the Board of Judges or Subcommittee, depending on the size of the award, is final.

9.0 Processing the Suggestion

The following are the steps and procedures to be used by each individual involved in preparing or processing a Suggestion form.

Originator

- Prepare Suggestion following directions printed on back of form.
- Submit the four-part form with Suggestion to Foreman or immediate Supervisor.

Supervisor

- Thank originator.
- Verify that employee has signed statement of acknowledgment of Terms/Rules of the Suggestion System.
- Read Suggestion.
- Sign Suggestion form and complete needed details.
- Determine if the nature and scope of the requested action is within your area of decision authority. If it is, analyze Suggestion recommendation and take appropriate action to implement or reject. Communicate with suggester where possible.
- If the requested action is not within your area of decision, forward completed form to proper investigating department. (The "appropriate investigator" is one who is in a position to evaluate the idea and, if acceptable, put it into effect.) If you are not sure, check by telephone with person you choose.
- Distribute four copies: Remove and forward the SUGGESTION SYSTEM copy immediately to the Suggestion Administrator and EMPLOYEE'S copy to suggester; file SUPERVISOR'S copy. ACTION copy to evaluator.
- Be impersonal during investigation and evaluation.

Note: Employee supervisor has the responsibility for follow-up on the investigation of suggestions for his employees.

Suggestion System Administrator

- Date SUGGESTION SYSTEM copy; complete data processing; and when returned, place in tickler file.

Person Possessing Decision Authority

If idea is acceptable:

- Enter a clear explanation of the decision in the space headed "Disposition." Sign and date.
- Perform (or cause to be performed) the required action to implement the idea. For example:

  Write Tool Order
  Write Maintenance Work Order
  Change Process Sheet(s)
  Write Purchase Requisition
  Write Memorandum, etc.

- After idea is installed, calculate savings and obtain IE (Industrial Engineering) verification.
- Return Suggestion to employee's Supervisor (not applicable if Supervisor accomplishes the disposition action).

If idea is not acceptable:

- Enter reason for not accepting in the space headed "Disposition."
- Return Suggestion to employee's Supervisor.

Supervisor

- Notify originator of action taken. If Suggestion is accepted, tell how his or her recommendation is being implemented. *Do not discuss any estimated potential savings or calculations prior to Suggestion System Committee action.* If not accepted, explain reason. Send both accepted and unapproved Suggestions back to the Suggestion System Administrator.

Suggestion Administrator

- Take approved Suggestions to the Subcommittees where they are accepted, rejected, returned for further information, or passed on to the Board of Judges.
- Notify management of awards of $100 or more for suitable publicity arrangements.
- File original Suggestion and keep for seven years from final decision date.

Nominal Group Technique
A Group Problem-Solving Process

Nominal group technique (NGT) is a structured form of brainstorming that has some special features:

• The process causes all of the group to be a part of the discussion and decisions.
• Everyone in the group is equal from the standpoint of sharing ideas.
• The process keeps dominant personalities in check.
• The results have a high chance of being successful.

NGT is a problem-solving process that works with task teams or quality circles. It is a powerful tool in almost any meeting. NGT is not a replacement for circles or teams, it is a tool to lead them to making better decisions. The process can be used two ways:

1. An NGT meeting can be called to resolve a problem prestated to the group. In this case, it is necessary to be sure that the group understands the task statement and that any needed modifications are made before it starts. The group is selected to include all of the thinking from various jobs involved in the task being analyzed. A good solution requires the input of all parties involved.

2. NGT can be used as the basic process for ongoing problem-solving teams. The team would use NGT as a method of identifying a range of problems that need investigation and prioritize the order on which they would be worked. The team would establish the task statement and usually wait until the next meeting for NGT analysis.

In both cases, it is best to let the group or team have several days to gather data relevant to the problem identified in the task statement. With some preparation, the results of NGT will be better.

It may be necessary to direct some data collection as a part of the meeting notice or after the voting in the first meeting on the task or problem. There is no reason that the decision must be made in the first meeting. Frequently there is the need for added data or the addition of added people that could bring a new perspective to the group.

Leading a Nominal Group Process

Group members:

• Six to 14 people
• Representing all aspects of the task
• Experienced in the task involved

Preparations:

• Meeting notice at least one week ahead of time stating task to be

discussed, time, place and any special instructions to group members.
- Meeting room large enough to accommodate group comfortably.
- Table arranged preferably in a U with the flipchart in middle or open end.

Supplies:

- Flipchart and paper, marking pens, voting cards, masking tape, tablet paper, and pencils.

Facilitator:

- Knows the NGT process.
- Assures that group follows process.
- Maintains control of group.
- Creates an open and cooperative atmosphere.

The facilitator opens the meeting by welcoming everyone in the group. If the group contains strangers, a round robin identifies each person by name, work area, and any data related to the task. A sign-up sheet should be circulated to get correct spelling of names, etc. The task statement is reviewed to be sure that all of the participants understand and agree with the content.

The facilitator reviews the rules of NGT:

1. During round-robin recording all ideas are accepted without challenge or comments. Clarification is done later.
2. Everyone should try to gain added ideas from other members' ideas. This is called piggybacking.
3. Clarification of ideas must come from the originator. The facilitator must prevent any ridicule of ideas.
4. All voting must be done in secret. The facilitator must prevent any pressures to control voting.

The Six Steps for Nominal Group Technique

Step 1. Task Statement
The task statement should be open-ended. This means that there is not a limit on the scope of the task and a solution is not preselected.

A task statement may be determined by the group from a listing of processes or products that the group feels could be improved for the benefit of the organization.

The task statement must have approval by the group.

Step 2. Silent Generation
Using the tablet paper provided, each group member spends five to 10 minutes identifying his or her answer to the task statement. There is to be no discussion during this time except to clarify the task statement.

The time allotted is specified before the group starts. The facilitator maintains silence and encourages those who finish early to do added thinking and not disturb others. If everyone in the group is done, the facilitator may move to the next step.

The facilitator can take part as an equal voting member or act as a professional resource to the group.

Step 3. Round-Robin Recording

Either the facilitator or a volunteer recorder will write down one idea from each group member in turn. The order of participation is strictly followed and only one idea per turn is accepted. The recording is done on the flipchart and the group member is asked if his or her idea is properly recorded. It is necessary to shorten many of the idea statements. This must be done with the approval of the source.

Do not force anyone to be a recorder. There is a threat of spelling competence and the risk of looking foolish. Also, some people will not willingly take on a recording task for a variety of reasons. It may be best for the facilitator to act as recorder.

It is permissible to say "pass" at any time and reenter the idea input at the next round. The facilitator should encourage group members to piggyback by finding new ideas from the ideas of others in the group. The process should not be threatening. It should be encouraging and fun. When all group members say "pass," the facilitator closes recording.

Step 4. Clarification

The recorder should first identify each idea with a letter (or number) to simplify reference to the ideas.

The facilitator should lead an open discussion to clarify each of the ideas and to combine them into fewer ideas where possible. The clarification should not become a vote promoting process. The person who originated the idea should not be placed in a role of defending his or her idea.

If the flipcharts are messed up, the remaining ideas should be transferred to a new page prior to voting. If possible, leave space ahead of each idea for the identifying letter and behind for the voting results. If the data are copied, hang the old charts on the wall so everyone is sure that no ideas were lost.

Step 5. Voting and Ranking

The facilitator has each person review the combined ideas and vote for the three that they think are the most important. Voting is to be done as a secret process using cards or similar paper. Voting gives 5 points for the first choice, 3 points for the second choice, and 1 point for the third choice. This spread of voting values helps spread out the results and provides more accurate data.

Each person completes his or her voting cards and turns them in to the facilitator or designated person. The facilitator assigns one or two of the group to read off the vote data so the results can be tallied on the flipchart.

Obtaining secret written votes eliminates any social pressures. Having one of the group call out the data prevents the vote being controlled by the leader. The posting of the ranking on the flipchart displays the results of all of the voting and generates consensus or ownership of the results. The mathematical process of voting and summing the votes increases the accuracy over a show-of-hands process.

If the voting is close and there is a large number of ideas with similar total ranking, it may be necessary to repeat the voting using only those with high scores. This will allow the group to focus on fewer ideas and rate them accordingly.

A preprinted voting card (Figure 5) is suggested rather than using blank 3-inch by 5-inch cards. The use of preprinted cards adds to the seriousness of the process and also helps maintain anonymity.

Step 6. *Discussion of Results*

The output of NGT is a list of ideas that covers a wide range of possibilities related to the original task statement. These ideas frequently need more data or inputs from added persons before the best response to the task statement can be selected.

If all the needed data and persons with vital inputs are present, then a final selection can be made with commitment by the entire group.

NGT will produce results that are accepted by the entire group and reflect the dynamics of group thinking. The structure of NGT carefully builds the acceptance of the process and the results.

Figure 5. Sample Voting Card

Cause and Effect Diagrams with Cards (CEDAC)
A Tool for Problem Solving in a Group Environment

Cause-and-effect diagrams with cards (CEDAC ® Productivity Inc.) are graphic tools which are very effective tools for use in problem analysis. The process utilizes both management expertise and worker knowhow in solving problems. It brings the improvement process out of the supervisor's office and onto the factory floor.

What is it?

Step-by-step group process for **problem solving:**
- Identifies facts
- Proposes solutions
- Tests solutions
- Documents effect on problem
- Participative approach, group consensus

Why use it?

Because it works.
- Makes problem visible
- Sets target and improvement measure
- Focuses on problem, instead of people
- Builds accurate and factual record of improvements
- Continues to work, overtime, to further reduce problems and improve the process.

CEDAC Diagram

Step 1 — Develop an Effect Statement

Write statement that describes and quantifies problem effect. Use numerical and historical data. Make statement visible on CEDAC diagram.

Step 2 — Determine an Improvement Measure

Decide on how to measure results of improvements, what data best measures results, how do we get the data and how often we measure. (The more the better.)

Step 3 — Determine a Target.

Develop a target statement.
- Target must be based on improvement measure. Target must have a date. (The sooner the better.)
- Make it visual. Complete effect (right) side of CEDAC diagram. At a minimum this should include the following:
  - Problem effect statement
  - Problem improvement measure
  - Target effect statement
  - Project Leader
  - Project start date
  - Target completion date

Step 4 — Generate fact-finding cards and post on diagram.

Facts about the problem are written on small colored cards. Avoid attempting to solve problem here. Just get the facts as you know them. Measurable facts are better than beliefs, but all are accepted. Facts go on left side of fishbone.

Step 5 — Generate improvement cards and post on diagram.

Improvement ideas are on different colored cards and posted on the opposite (right) side of fishbone. All improvement ideas are accepted, but they must be written on improvement cards. Synthesize similar cards as needed and categorize them on major trunks of diagram.

Step 6 — Select and test improvement ideas.

Members review and evaluate improvement ideas. Try to get consensus on ideas to test. Members mark cards with dot to signify their acceptance. Manager still retains final authority for test and installation. Try only one idea at a time. Post results of improvement, either good or bad.

Step 7 Incorporate successful improvement ideas.

Display improvement card for recognition. Repeat steps 3 through 6 until target is reached.

Design of Experiments
A Tool for Product or Process Problem Solving

Experiments are a forceful tool in optimizing a product or a process. A body of knowledge known as "Design of Experiments" is available to improve the process of experimentation. It has been used extensively in many countries, and was an important factor in Japan's successful production of high quality products at low cost. This illustration outlines the basic steps involved in the "Design of Experiments" approach to solving problems.

What is it?

A body of knowledge intended to improve the process of learning from experimentation.

Why use it?

- It quickly optimizes product designs and production process
- Reduces Testing Costs
- Faster development cycles
- Improved Design to Production Transition
- Improved supplier product quality

Results

- The optimum of product designs or production processes
- The most stable of production processes
- Lowest cost test program

Step 1 — Determine Experiment Design

A. Use brainstorming or NGT to determine:
  - Choice of variables
  - Choice of responses
  - Levels of each variables
  - Potential non-linearities
  - Possible variable interactions
  - Measurement techniques
  - Potential execution problems

B. Select experiment design

Step 2

Perform experiments and study data to determine what results are statistically significant, and if the experiment assumptions are correct.

Step 3 — Design optimization experiments

Select appropriate experiment design.

Step 4

Perform optimization experiments and analyze data to determine the best set of variables or the direction to the optimum conditions of variables.

Ergonomics (Human Factors Engineering)
A Tool for Achieving Improvement in the Workplace

Ergonomics matches human capabilities and limitations to the work place and the systems they operate and maintain. The objective of Ergonomics is to make it easier for our employees to do their jobs and for our customers to operate and maintain our products.

What is it?

- An engineering discipline to improve worker productivity, quality and safety by ergonomic design of product or work place.
- Analysis of a task in terms of human capabilities.
- Adjustment of the work environment to fit human needs.

Why use it?

- Improve quality of work through greater productivity and quality.
- Improve quality of work life due to happier workers, less stress and fatigue.
- Improve safety through fewer accidents, injuries, lost time, etc.

ERGONOMICS IS THE INTERACTION OF THE

TASK

WORKER

ENVIRONMENT (HEAT, LIGHT, SOUND)

Step 1
Determine what information is needed to perform task(s).

Step 2
Determine what actions the user needs to perform task(s).

Step 3
Develop functional requirements (top level) for the human-environment interface.
- Tells what must be done under what condition, but not how to do it.

Step 4
Allocate functions between human and automation.

Step 5
Conduct performance trade-off analyses on display and control technologies.
- Use functional requirements as a guide.

Step 6
Develop work station requirements stating the boundary conditions for each display and control.
- Examples: Display brightness
  Control force
  Environmental constraints

Step 7
Perform a work space or product layout. Specify locations of operator display(s) and control(s).

Step 8
For electronic displays, define:
- Information format
- Highlighting techniques
- Error messaging
- Feedback to user
- Timing of information presentation

Input/Output Analysis A Tool for Improving the Definition of Roles, Responsibilities and Interdependencies

Input/output analysis is a systematic way of identifying interdependency problems by defining objectives, then listing the inputs and outputs for major tasks, functions or individuals. Input/output analysis can be effective for a function, group, department or program. The illustration shows the steps in the process.

What is it?

It's a group process for:

- Defining or redefining roles and responsibilities
- Defining or redefining interfaces between team members
- Solving problems relating to either of the above.

Why use it?

It produces a more harmonious and clear-cut understanding of roles and responsibilities, and:

- Resolves conflicts
- Eliminates duplications
- Opens lines of communication.

Step 1 — Back to Basics

Define

- Program objectives/deliverables
- Work breakdown structure
- Master schedule
- Organization chart
- Other relevant program information (i.e., funding, subcontractors, GFE, etc.)

Step 2 — Responsibilities

Establish each team member's prime and support responsibilities

- List major program tasks
- List people responsible
- Identify who has (P) Prime and (S) Support responsibility

Step 3 — Input/Output

Define each team member's role.

- Write a brief job description
- List specific major tasks
- Define inputs and outputs for each task
- Define interface personnel by name
- Work with team members to resolve any conflicts

Step 4 — Ideas for Improvement

Where are we today?

- Identify ideas that could help the program better meet performance, schedule and cost objectives
- Prioritize
- Develop action plan
- Establish responsibilities
- Set completion dates
- Use NGT process

Step 5 — Implementation

- Implement the new, clear-cut job and task descriptions
- Follow the input/output actions listed
- Delegate individual program responsibilities
- Implement action plan

Step 6 — Follow-up

- Measure individual and team performance
- Set new goals
- Measure and follow-up new goals
- Repeat steps 2 through 5 for each phase of the program, or every six months

Just-in-Time (JIT)
A Pull Rather than a Push Manufacturing Control System

Just-in-Time (JIT) is a pull type manu-facturing control system that provides:

- The right material
- At the right place
- At the right time.

The system emphasizes problem solv-ing and utilizes employee involvement and group process techniques.

What is it?

It is a pull type manufacturing process that involves:

- Enforced problem solving
- "Right the first time" philosophy
- Pull rather than push system
- Linear scheduling

Why use it?

The JIT system forces waste elimination by:

- Requiring a higher quality product
- Reducing lot size and inventories
- Reducing set-up times

Note: JIT is a form of process cycle time reduction, and can be applied to processes other than manufacturing.

J.I.T.

REDUCED INVENTORIES

Exposes Quality Problems → Quality Problem Elimination → Waste Prevention

Small Lot Production → Further Lot Size Reductions

Enhances Quality Assurance → Fast Detection Fast Correction → Waste Reduction

Improved JIT Performance

Improved Quality

Step 1 — Establish the team/goal/vision

- Establish team of supervision, operators and engineers.
- Establish culture of do-it-once, do-it-right. Shut line down if something is not right.
- Establish goals/vision
  - Material is either moving between operation or is having value added.
  - Small lot sizes (1 is ideal).
  - Zero defects is a realizable goal.
  - Rework, scrap, inspection, stocking, set-up, inventories are all waste to be eliminated.

Step 2 — Define the Process Flow

- Develop a flowchart.
- Estimate process cycle time.
- Balance line with staff/facilities.
- Use team approach.

Step 3 — Identify yields and improvement actions

- Identify yield of each step in process.
- Use Pareto technique to determine which step to fix first.
- Implement continuous improvement actions to improve yields.

Step 4 — Install a Linear Scheduling System

- Must accomplish the same amount from each operation/shift.
- Self-scheduling visually obvious.

Nominal Group Technique/Brainstorming
A Tool for Idea Generation and Problem Solving

Using nominal group technique (NGT), a group of employees (workers, supervisors, managers) work together to identify problem areas. Everyone participates in this process, which isolates specific problems quickly. The illustration shows the process in detail.

What is it?

It's a group process for identifying:

- Ideas
- Solutions
- Issues
- Problems

It's a proactive search process

All participants contribute equally

Why use it?

It produces many ideas/solutions in a short time

It focuses on problems, not people

It opens the lines of communication within a group

It ensures participation

It tolerates conflicting ideas

It captures creative ideas

Ground Rules

1. Do not judge or editorialize or editorialize
2. Allow no members to judge or editorialize
3. Stay with "round robin" turns so no one is missed
4. Do not overlook shy people, nor let aggressive/informal leaders dominate
5. Instruct people to make own decisions about redundant ideas. If someone' calls out an idea on a participant's list, that participant should cross it off his or her list. If the thought is significantly different and merits consideration, the participant should call it out on a turn. It is the participant's decision to make.

Step 1 — The NGT Process in Action.

Group leader addresses subject, presents the problem/issue to be dealt with by the group. Gives instructions.

Step 2 — Idea generation. Silent writing.

- Participants seated at tables
- Participants have paper and pencil
- Participants write out whatever ideas "pop" into their heads
- 10-15 minutes for writing
- Leader has flipchart
- Leader may participate

Step 3 — Idea gathering. Leader conducts "round robin."

- Each person contributes an idea in turn
- Leader may participate in turn
- Ideas written on flip chart
- All ideas written as stated
- Post all filled pages for all to view
- Continue until each person passes
- Participants may delete ideas from list
- Participants may add ideas
- No evaluation/judgment by leader or participant
- Review complete list for priority ranking

At this point leader may restate general issue or problem under consideration.

Step 4 — Process/Clarify Ideas

- Each item discussed
- Some combined, new ideas added
- Every participant understands ideas

Step 5 — Priority Setting

Participants silently examine clarified items

- Participants silently select their top 3, 5 or 7 (about 20-25% of list)
- Participants call out their top priority items
- Record tally on flipchart

Step 6
Action Plan

- Review top five priority items
- Develop consensus on who will develop action
- Set completion date for plan

Statistical Process Control
A Tool for Solving Problems and Improving Performance

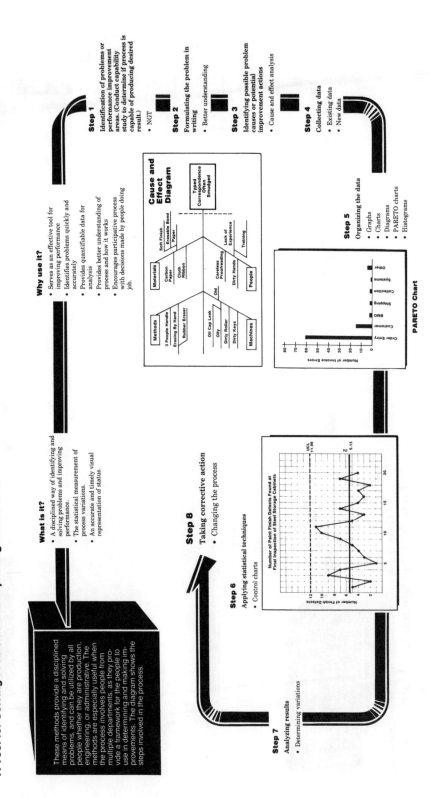

These methods provide a disciplined means of identifying and solving problems, and can be utilized by all people whether they are production, engineering, or administrative. The methods are especially useful when the process involves people from multiple departments, as they provide a framework for the people to use in determining and making improvements. The diagram shows the steps involved in the process.

What is it?
- A disciplined way of identifying and solving problems and improving performance.
- The statistical measurement of process variations.
- An accurate and timely visual representation of status.

Why use it?
- Serves as an effective tool for improving performance
- Identifies problems quickly and accurately
- Provides quantifiable data for analysis
- Provides better understanding of process and how it works
- Encourages participative process with decisions made by people doing job.

Step 1
Identification of problems or performance improvement areas. (Conduct capability study to determine if process is capable of producing desired result.)
- NGT

Step 2
Formulating the problem in writing
- Better understanding

Step 3
Identifying possible problem causes or potential improvement actions
- Cause and effect analysis

Step 4
Collecting data
- Existing data
- New data

Step 5
Organizing the data
- Graphs
- Charts
- Diagrams
- PARETO charts
- Histograms

Step 6
Applying statistical techniques
- Control charts

Step 7
Analyzing results
- Determining variations

Step 8
Taking corrective action
- Changing the process

Cause and Effect Diagram

Materials: Soft Finish, Erasable Bond Paper, Carbon Paper, Cloth Ribbon

People: Lack of Experience, Training, Careless Proofreading, Dirty Hands

Methods: 3 People Handle, Erasing By Hand, Rubber Eraser

Machines: Oil Cap Leak, Oily, Old, Dirty Roller, Dirty Keys

Typed Correspondence Often Smudged

PARETO Chart

Number of Invoice Errors (0–80): Order Entry, Customer, BMO, Shipping, Collection, Systems, Other

Number of Paint Finish Defects Found at Final Inspection of Steel Storage Cabinets

UCL 11.98

x̄ 5.15

Number of Finish Defects

Teambuilding
A Tool for Improving Team Performance

A team is a group of people working together for a common goal when accomplishment of that goal requires interdependence. In organizations it is often the case that to get the job done we need to work together as a team.

Because of this need to work in a team atmosphere, leaders and managers need to work on the development and maintenance of the team — this is called teambuilding. Members of teams look to the leader to provide them help working in the team environment.

Teambuilding is a regular part of any team leader's job. As you develop your work plan, plan time for teambuilding activities. It may head off schedule problems, cost problems, misunderstandings and confusion later on. It is a good investment of your time as a manager or team leader.

What is it?

Teambuilding is the process of developing and maintaining a group of people who are working together for a common goal.

Why use it?

Often the accomplishment of a goal requires interdependence. To get the job done we need to work together as a team.

Ground rules

1. Don't ignore team/team member problems. Think through the symptoms and uncover the cause(s). Focus on the problem not on personalities.
2. Maintain a balance between the needs of the individuals, the team, and the goal.

The Process In Action:

Step 1
Identify the team.

The team ideally should be made up of people who share a common goal which requires an interdependence.

Step 2
Develop the Team.

- Develop and maintain team trust, respect and dignity for all members.
- Locate people in the same area if possible.
- Develop a team identity (a logo, team name, etc.).
- Set aside a social time so team members can get to know each other.
- Discuss how members are or are not working together in an open and non-threatening way.

Step 3
Identify the Team Goals.

- Goals should be set in a participative manner as much as possible. The NGT process can be used.
- The team goals and priorities must be understood and accepted by the members.
- Ensure members are clear in what their contributions are and with whom they need to interface.

Step 4 — Recognize team accomplishments regularly, publically and privately. Teams, like individuals, want to do a good job and need to feel that their contributions are important.

Step 5
Maintain the Team.

Teams are a living entity and thus change with time. In order for a team to continue to be successful it must recognize and cope with change. To do this, repeat steps 2, 3, and 4 as necessary.

VALUE ANALYSIS (VE/VA Value Engineering/Value Analysis)
A TOOL FOR IMPROVING PROCESSES and PRODUCTS

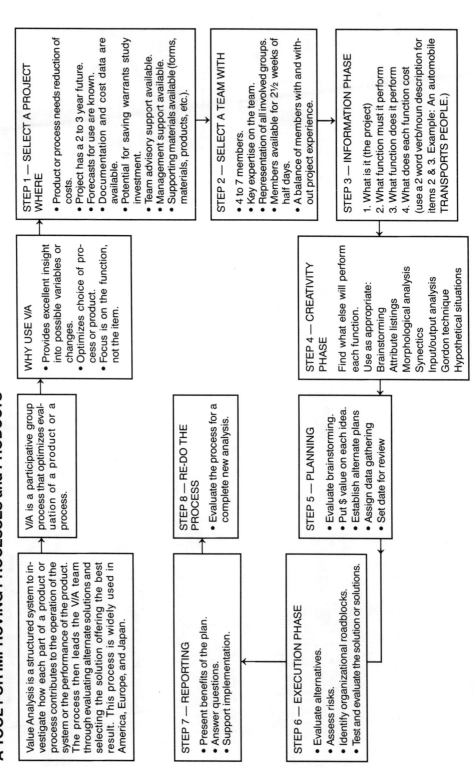

Value Analysis is a structured system to investigate how each part of a product or process contributes to the operation of the system or the performance of the product. The process then leads the V/A team through evaluating alternate solutions and selecting the solution offering the best result. This process is widely used in America, Europe, and Japan.

V/A is a participative group process that optimizes evaluation of a product or a process.

WHY USE V/A
- Provides excellent insight into possible variables or changes.
- Optimizes choice of process or product.
- Focus is on the function, not the item.

STEP 1 — SELECT A PROJECT WHERE
- Product or process needs reduction of costs.
- Project has a 2 to 3 year future.
- Forecasts for use are known.
- Documentation and cost data are available.
- Potential for saving warrants study investment.
- Team advisory support available.
- Management support available.
- Supporting materials available (forms, materials, products, etc.).

STEP 2 — SELECT A TEAM WITH
- 4 to 7 members.
- Key expertise on the team.
- Representation of all involved groups.
- Members available for 2½ weeks of half days.
- A balance of members with and without project experience.

STEP 3 — INFORMATION PHASE
1. What is it (the project)
2. What function must it perform
3. What function does it perform
4. What does each function cost
(use a 2 word verb/noun description for items 2 & 3. Example: An automobile TRANSPORTS PEOPLE.)

STEP 4 — CREATIVITY PHASE
Find what else will perform each function.
Use as appropriate:
Brainstorming
Attribute listings
Morphological analysis
Synectics
Input/output analysis
Gordon technique
Hypothetical situations

STEP 5 — PLANNING
- Evaluate brainstorming.
- Put $ value on each idea.
- Establish alternate plans
- Assign data gathering
- Set date for review

STEP 6 — EXECUTION PHASE
- Evaluate alternatives.
- Assess risks.
- Identify organizational roadblocks.
- Test and evaluate the solution or solutions.

STEP 7 — REPORTING
- Present benefits of the plan.
- Answer questions.
- Support implementation.

STEP 8 — RE-DO THE PROCESS
- Evaluate the process for a complete new analysis.

Visual Controls
A Tool for Better Control of Work Processes

Simple, but effective visual aids that:
- Improve the Process, Process Control, and Process Safety, and/or
- Provide a means to track and control performance in a working group or department.

What is it?

Visual controls and visual aids that improve:
- Process
- Control of process
- Process safety

Why use it?

- Better communications
- Quick and efficient process management
- Immediate identification of in-process materials, salvage, or scrap
- Safer work environment
- Neat work place
- Faster process times

... WARNING LIGHTS, MARKED GAUGES, FLOOR DESIGNATOR, TOOL RACKS, MOUNTING ASSEMBLIES, COLOR CODED CONTAINERS, WARNINGS, ETC., ETC.

Results

- A better place to work.
- Higher productivity and a better quality of products.

Step 1 — Determine where to apply visual controls.

Use brainstorming or NGT to determine where visual controls are useful or required.

Step 2 — Set Priorities.

Select those visual controls required, or most useful — those that will provide for better safety or greater quality and productivity.

Step 3 — Develop Action Plan.

- Determine action needed to effect improvements
- Determine who is responsible for the completion of each action and when.

VISUAL CONTROLS		
WHAT	WHO	WHEN

Work Flow Analysis (WFA)
A Tool for Achieving Improvement in Processes

What is it?

A participative group process for eliminating unnecessary tasks and streamlining the work flow.

Work flow analysis is a structured system to improve any work process by eliminating unnecessary tasks and streamlining the work flow. This analysis is particularly good for specific functions and/or departments where a problem has already been identified. The illustration shows the steps of work flow analysis.

Why use it?

The WFA process:

- Simplifies work
- Shortens troublesome processes
- Improves performance

Step 1 — Obtain Commitment for Analysis Project

- Management
- Department
- Individual
- Team Concept

Step 2 — Define the Process in Terms of:

- Process purposes
- Process objectives
- Process start and end points

Step 3 — List Process by Elements Including:

- Responsible party index
- Actual and elapsed time
- Flowchart symbol

Step 4 — Analyze the Process

- Use nominal group technique
- Microcomputer-assisted flowchart generation
- Question —
  Are all the listed steps necessary?
  Which steps are labor intensive?
  Does duplication of effort exist?
  Is the process flow logical?

Step 5 — Determine and Implement an Action Plan

- Select improvement tasks
- Assign specific responsibilities
- Establish goals
- Measure results

Step 6 Follow-up Actions

- Facilitator monitored
- Reported to team

WORK FLOW ANALYSIS

OBTAIN COMMITMENT

DEFINE PROCESS

LIST PROCESS

ANALYZE PROCESS

ACTION PLAN

WFA PROCESS ELEMENTAL LISTING

IDEA IDENTIFICATION WORKSHEET

IDEA ACTION PLAN

Measuring Performance

How are we doing? Did we meet our plan? How much have we improved? To determine the answers to these questions and others, we need to use measurements as yardsticks. With comparisons of past, present, and projected performance, we can measure our changes.

More importantly, measurements show us where to take action, and they evaluate the actions already taken. They give us the information we need to:

- Determine progress against plan, goals and needs.
- Identify problems or changes as they occur so corrective action can be taken.
- Evaluate the extent and effectiveness of changes and improvements.
- Motivate people and increase job satisfaction. People pay more attention to measurements when progress can then be seen and felt.
- Determine and evaluate trends.

Although measurements are effective aids to performance improvement, they are not infallible. The best measurements do not attempt too much or claim too much. It's the people who solve problems, not the measurements. But the right measurements can tell people where to apply their problem-solving skills.

Types of Measurements

To determine progress, different types of measurements must be conducted at different levels of the organization. In all cases, improvement is the objective of measurement, not measurement for its own sake.

Measurements can be broken down into two basic categories — macro-measurements and micro-measurements.

Macro-Measurements

Macro-measurements are used at the divisional, operational, and functional levels, and are capable of being added to give totals. These totals indicate performance trends and, while not giving the reasons for changes, show where further analysis is needed. The totals cannot be used to compare operations or divisions since the nature of their business dictates that there will be differences. However, if a division's trend varies greatly from the others, the macro-measurement will suggest a closer look to determine the cause.

Micro-Measurements

Micro-measurements are done at the department or work group level to improve productivity and quality of work. These measurements must be developed, agreed upon, and used as a diagnostic tool by the people actually doing the work. Measurement without ownership is worse than no measurement at all.

To be effective, micro-measurements must have the following characteristics:

- They must be developed and followed by the people doing the work being measured.
- They must be periodic to indicate changes as they occur.
- They must be applied to groups or processes.
- Their results must be analyzed by those who can influence and are responsible for those results.
- They may consist of a family of related measurements with understood limitations. This is more useful than trying to find one all-inclusive measurement.

Examples of Micro-Measurements by Function

Production

$$\frac{\text{Direct Hours}}{\text{Standard Hours}}$$

$$\frac{\text{Earned Hours}}{\text{Direct Hours}}$$

$$\frac{\text{Indirect Hours}}{\text{Direct Hours}}$$

$$\frac{\text{Salvage Hours}}{\text{Direct Hours}}$$

$$\frac{\text{Set-up Hours}}{\text{Earned Hours}}$$

$$\frac{\text{Direct Labor \$}}{\text{Standard Hours}}$$

$$\frac{\text{\#Units Accepted}}{\text{\#Units Inspected}}$$

$$\frac{\text{Wait Time Hours}}{\text{Direct Labor Hours}}$$

$$\frac{\text{Units Scheduled}}{\text{Units Produced}}$$

$$\frac{\text{Complete Kits Issued}}{\text{Total Kits Issued}}$$

$$\frac{\text{Cost of Sales}}{\text{Gross Inventory}}$$

$$\frac{\text{Scrap Costs}}{\text{LBM Additions}}$$

$$\frac{\text{LBM \& Support Costs}}{\text{\# Units Produced}}$$

$$\frac{\text{Fixed Price Cost of Sales}}{\text{Gross Net Inventory}}$$

$$\frac{\text{Sales/VA Sales}}{\text{Direct Headcount}}$$

$$\frac{\text{Sales/VA Sales}}{\text{Total Headcount}}$$

$$\frac{\text{Product Build \& Support Hours}}{\text{Equivalent Units Produced}}$$

$$\frac{\text{Customer Accepted Lots}}{\text{Lots Submitted}}$$

$$\frac{\text{Warranty Repair Costs}}{\text{Sales}}$$

$$\frac{\text{Sales/VA Sales}}{\text{Indirect Headcount}}$$

$$\frac{\text{Cost of Quality}}{\text{Cost of Sales}}$$

$$\frac{\text{PBIT}}{\text{Employees}}$$

$$\frac{\text{Act. Process Cycle Time}}{\text{Base Process Cycle Time}}$$

$$\frac{\text{Inventory Shortage}}{\text{Inventory Additions}}$$

$$\frac{\text{Total Production Hours}}{\text{Direct Earned Hours}}$$

Examples of Micro-Measurements by Function (cont.)

Production

$$\frac{\text{Delinquent Units } x \text{ Selling Price}}{\textit{Average Daily Sales}}$$

$$\frac{\text{Production Support Costs}}{\textit{Production LBM Costs}}$$

$$\frac{\text{Indirect Headcount}}{\textit{Direct Headcount}}$$

$$\frac{\text{Production Hourly Headcount}}{\textit{Production Control Headcount}}$$

$$\frac{\text{Production Hourly Headcount}}{\textit{Production Engineering Headcount}}$$

$$\frac{\text{\# Defects}}{\textit{\# Units Inspected}}$$

$$\frac{\text{Hours on Labor Ticket Rejects}}{\textit{Total Hours Reported}}$$

$$\frac{\text{Actual Burden Rate}}{\textit{Planned Burden Rate}}$$

$$\frac{\text{\# Personnel Transfers}}{\textit{Headcount}}$$

$$\frac{\text{Prod. Lines on JIT}}{\textit{Total Prod. Lines}}$$

Engineering

$$\frac{\text{\# Std. Parts in Releases}}{\textit{Total \# Parts in Releases}}$$

$$\frac{\text{Direct Labor}}{\textit{Total Time Reporting Labor}}$$

$$\frac{\text{Sales/VA Sales}}{\textit{Time Reporting Headcount}}$$

$$\frac{\text{Sales/VA Sales}}{\textit{Indirect Headcount}}$$

$$\frac{\text{Sales/VA Sales}}{\textit{Total Headcount}}$$

$$\frac{\text{\# Software Instructions}}{\textit{\# Software Engineers}}$$

$$\frac{\text{Cost to Prepare Drawings}}{\textit{\# Drawings Produced}}$$

$$\frac{\text{Prod. Build Hrs. On Layouts}}{\textit{Prod. Build Hrs.}}$$

$$\frac{\text{PBIT}}{\textit{Employees}}$$

$$\frac{\text{Actual Burden Rate}}{\textit{Planned Burden Rate}}$$

$$\frac{\text{\# Personnel Transfer}}{\textit{Headcount}}$$

$$\frac{\text{Projected Unit Build Cost}}{\textit{Target Unit Build Cost}}$$

$$\frac{\text{Production Support Costs}}{\textit{Production LBM Costs}}$$

$$\frac{\text{\# ECOs}}{\textit{\# Drawings}}$$

$$\frac{\text{Hrs. on Rejected Time Reports}}{\textit{Total Hrs. Reported}}$$

$$\frac{\text{Projects with Plans}}{\textit{Total Projects}}$$

$$\frac{\text{Projects Overrun \$}}{\textit{Total Projects \$}}$$

$$\frac{\text{CAD Hours Usage}}{\textit{CAD Hours Available}}$$

$$\frac{\text{\# Progs. w/OTPT Plans}}{\textit{Total \# Progs.}}$$

Examples of Micro-Measurements by Function (cont.)

Engineering (cont.)

$$\frac{\text{\# Prog. w/DTUPC}}{\textit{Total \# Progs.}}$$

$$\frac{\text{Milestones Completed ITD}}{\textit{Milestones Scheduled ITD}}$$

$$\frac{\text{\# Key Performance Specs Met}}{\textit{Total \# Key Performance Specs}}$$

$$\frac{\text{\# Drawings}}{\textit{Drafting Headcount}}$$

$$\frac{\text{\# ECOs}}{\textit{\# Engineers}}$$

$$\frac{\text{Bid Hours}}{\textit{Estimated Hours}}$$

$$\frac{\text{Negotiated Hours}}{\textit{Bid Hours}}$$

$$\frac{\text{Planned Cost All Progams}}{\textit{Actual Cost All Programs}}$$

$$\frac{\text{Factory Costs}}{\textit{Production Engineering Costs}}$$

Service Engineering

$$\frac{\text{\$ Orders Received YTD}}{\textit{\$ Orders Planned YTD}}$$

$$\frac{\text{\$ Order Received} \cdot \text{Month/Year}}{\textit{\# Marketeers/Contract Admin.}}$$

$$\frac{\text{Total Operations Personnel}}{\textit{Service Engineering Personnel}}$$

$$\frac{\text{Sales/VA Sales}}{\textit{Service Engineering Headcount}}$$

$$\frac{\text{Operations Budget}}{\textit{Service Engineering Budget}}$$

$$\frac{\text{\$ Delinquent Deliveries}}{\textit{Average Daily Sales}}$$

$$\frac{\text{\# Proposals}}{\textit{\# Marketing Reps.}}$$

$$\frac{\text{\$ Orders Received}}{\textit{Service Engineering Budget}}$$

$$\frac{\text{\# Active Contracts}}{\textit{\# Contract Administrators}}$$

$$\frac{\text{FP Orders with Progress Payments}}{\textit{Total \# FP Orders}}$$

$$\frac{\text{Sales Proposal \$}}{\textit{\$ Orders Received}}$$

$$\frac{\text{Proposals Submitted}}{\textit{Proposals Won}}$$

$$\frac{\text{Service Engineering Budget}}{\textit{Operations Sales}}$$

Examples of Micro-Measurements by Function (cont.)

Human Resources

$$\frac{\text{Change Notices Processed}}{\text{\# Compensation Clericals}}$$

$$\frac{\text{Sales/VA Sales}}{\text{Employee Relations Headcount}}$$

$$\frac{\text{Total Operations Headcount}}{\text{Employee Relations Headcount}}$$

$$\frac{\text{\# Change Notice Errors}}{\text{Total Change Notices}}$$

$$\frac{\text{\# People Interviewed \& Hired}}{\text{\# People Interviewed}}$$

$$\frac{\text{Operations Support}}{\text{Employee Relations Budget}}$$

$$\frac{\text{Elapsed Time of Unprocessed ECRs}}{\text{\# Unprocessed ECRs}}$$

$$\frac{\text{Insurance Claims Processed}}{\text{\# Insurance Claim Clerks}}$$

$$\frac{\text{Lost Time for Injuries}}{\text{Total Hours Worked}}$$

$$\frac{\text{Workers Compensation Costs}}{\text{Total Hours Worked}}$$

$$\frac{\text{Offers Made}}{\text{Offers Accepted}}$$

$$\frac{\text{Employees Terminating}}{\text{Total Employees}}$$

$$\frac{\text{Satisfied Employees}}{\text{Total Employees}}$$

Information Systems

$$\frac{\text{Output Distributed On Time}}{\text{Total Output Distributed}}$$

$$\frac{\text{Hardware Uptime}}{\text{Total Hardware Time}}$$

$$\frac{\text{Out of Service Terminals}}{\text{Total \# Terminals}}$$

$$\frac{\text{Trouble Calls Received}}{\text{Unit of Time (Week, Mo., Etc.)}}$$

$$\frac{\text{Keypunch Earned Hours}}{\text{Keypunch Actual Hours}}$$

$$\frac{\text{Jobs Completed}}{\text{Jobs Scheduled}}$$

$$\frac{\text{Sales/VA Sales}}{\text{IS Headcount}}$$

$$\frac{\text{Total Operations Headcount}}{\text{IS Headcount}}$$

$$\frac{\text{Operations Budget}}{\text{IS Budget}}$$

$$\frac{\text{User Complaints}}{\text{Hours of Usage}}$$

$$\frac{\text{Proj. Estimated Development Cost}}{\text{Proj. Actual Development Cost}}$$

$$\frac{\text{IS Cost}}{\text{Revenue}}$$

$$\frac{\text{\# Terminals}}{\text{\# Employees}}$$

Examples of Micro-Measurements by Function (cont.)

Product Assurance

$$\frac{\text{PA Dept. Hours}}{\text{Production Hours}}$$

$$\frac{\text{PA Indirect Hours}}{\text{Total Quality Hours}}$$

$$\frac{\text{Earned Hours}}{\text{Direct Hours}}$$

$$\frac{\text{Cost of Quality}}{\text{Cost of Sales}}$$

$$\frac{\text{Sales/VA Sales}}{\text{Product Assurance Headcount}}$$

$$\frac{\text{Total Receiving Insp. Hours}}{\text{Lots Received}}$$

$$\frac{\text{Material Lots Inspected}}{\text{Receiving Inspection Headcount}}$$

$$\frac{\text{Total Operating Headcount}}{\text{PA Dept. Headcount}}$$

$$\frac{\text{Operations Budget}}{\text{PA Dept. Budget}}$$

$$\frac{\text{Production Earned Hours}}{\text{Quality Eng. Support Hours}}$$

$$\frac{\text{QE Support Costs}}{\text{Production LBM Costs}}$$

$$\frac{\text{Errors on Inspection Procedures}}{\text{Inspection Procedures Issued}}$$

$$\frac{\text{Errors in Data Collection}}{\text{Volume of Data Collected}}$$

$$\frac{\text{Actual Burden Rate}}{\text{Planned Burden Rate}}$$

$$\frac{\text{Prevention Costs}}{\text{Cost of Quality}}$$

$$\frac{\text{Appraisal Costs}}{\text{Cost of Quality}}$$

$$\frac{\text{Failure Costs}}{\text{Cost of Quality}}$$

$$\frac{\text{\# QEs on Engr. Progs.}}{\text{Total \# QEs}}$$

Material

$$\frac{\text{Purchase Order Errors}}{\text{Purchase Orders Audited}}$$

$$\frac{\text{Estimated Savings on Orders Placed}}{\text{Dollar Value of Orders Placed}}$$

$$\frac{\text{Material Proposal Records Received}}{\text{Material Proposal Records Completed}}$$

$$\frac{\text{Incoming Material Lots Accepted}}{\text{Incoming Material Lots}}$$

$$\frac{\text{\$ Amount of Purchases}}{\text{Purchasing Dept. Headcount}}$$

$$\frac{\text{Procurement Dept. Budget}}{\text{Purchase Orders Issued}}$$

Examples of Micro-Measurements by Function (cont.)

Material (cont.)

# POs Placed	Sales/VA Sales	Vendor Lots on Time
Purchasing Dept. Headcount	*Procurement Dept. Headcount*	*Vendor Lots Received*

Total Operations Headcount	$ Amount of Purchases	
Purchasing Dept. Headcount	*Purchasing Dept. Budget*	

Communications

Reproduction Costs	Sales/VA Sales	Cost of Viewgraph Change
# Pages Produced	*Communications Dept. Headcount*	*Total Graphics Cost*

Viewgraphs Redone	Operations Headcount	
Total Viewgraphs Produced	*Communications Dept. Headcount*	

Finance

Trade Billed Receivables	Operations Budget	Finance Dept. Budget
Avg. Trade Billed Sales/Day	*Finance Dept. Budget*	*Sales*

Invoices Processed x Standard	Sales/VA Sales	$ Value of Pricing Proposal
Disbursement Audit Hours	*Finance Personnel*	*# Pricing People*

Total Operations Personnel	Profit Dollars	Invoicing Errors
Finance Personnel	*Payroll Dollars*	*Invoices Processed*

Net Assets	Receivables Over 60 Days	Customer Satisfaction Index Net Billings
Sales	*Total Receivables*	*Indirect Headcount*

# Pricing Proposals	Incomplete Cost Standard	
# Pricing People	*Total Cost Standards*	

Examples of Micro-Measurements by Function (cont.)

General/Miscellaneous

$$\frac{\text{Actual Hrs./\$}}{\text{Estimated Hrs./\$}}$$

$$\frac{\text{Direct Headcount}}{\text{Indirect Headcount}}$$

$$\frac{\text{Operations Headcount}}{\text{Department Headcount}}$$

$$\frac{\text{Operations Sales/VA Sales}}{\text{Department Headcount}}$$

$$\frac{\text{Building Sq. Footage}}{\text{Maintenance Cleaning Personnel}}$$

$$\frac{\text{Maintenance Orders Within Estimate}}{\text{Total Maintenance Orders}}$$

$$\frac{\text{Unplanned Absent Hours}}{\text{Total Hours}}$$

$$\frac{\text{Pages Produced}}{\text{Word Processing Headcount}}$$

$$\frac{\text{Backlog Hrs. on Maintenance Work Orders}}{\text{Maintenance Headcount}}$$

$$\frac{\text{Non-Productive Time}}{\text{Total Time Available}}$$

$$\frac{\text{Department Costs}}{\text{Department Budgeted Costs}}$$

$$\frac{\text{Headcount}}{\text{\# Secretaries}}$$

$$\frac{\text{\# People in QC Teams}}{\text{Total Employees}}$$

$$\frac{\text{Sales}}{\text{Assets}}$$

$$\frac{\text{Profit}}{\text{Employees}}$$

$$\frac{\text{Facilities Cost}}{\text{Facilities Sq. Ft.}}$$

$$\frac{\text{Assets}}{\text{Employees}}$$

Performance Improvement Process

Performance improvement is a continuous process. It requires a commitment at all levels — individual, group, department, and division — and in all job functions

The guide establishes seven steps, or sequential actions, you must take to improve performance. Each of them will lead you in the right direction toward achieving quality of work, quality of work life and quality of management. This diagram summarizes the seven action improvement steps.

Action 1. Establishing the Management and Cultural Environment

The first step that affects this whole process is establishing the needed environment to effect change. The guidelines give steps to follow in involving others in an effective way to bring about performance improvement.

Action 2. Defining the Mission

It's important that the action group delineates its reason for existence, its purpose for continuing in business, and a list of its products and services. To be effective they must be doing the right things as well as doing things right.

Action 3. Set Performance Improvement Goals

Assess your current performance level competitive position, vision of the future, and your present goals. Then define your overall improvement goals before you choose your specific performance improvement project(s) and the mini-goals associated with it.

Action 4. Establish Improvement Plans

Determine what aspects need improvement, how much you should change, and when it is necessary to change. Look at your group from a "perfect world model" and a "cost driver" viewpoint. Then define plans for improvement.

Action 5. Implement Projects Utilizing Performance Improvement Tools

Employ the fundamental elements of good management in promoting performance improvements. And make use of the many tools available to you to ensure that you improve performance successfully.

Action 6. Measuring Results

Develop ongoing measurements that keep track of your progress against your mini-goals as well as your ultimate goal. Be sure that these measurements are easy to understand, and effectively provide an indication of success or failure.

Action 7. Track Results and Take Corrective Action

To determine your planned progress against plan, compare your results with your goals. Take corrective actions wherever your goals are not being met.

Glossary

This glossary summarizes the terms, acronyms, and processes used in the book. It provides some sources for help — both books and consultants, but does not include *all* the terms, books, or consultants. It reflects books I have found useful, and consultants from which I have learned or with which I am familiar.

Cause-and-Effect Diagram

Sometimes called an Ishikawa diagram or a fishbone diagram. First used by Ishikawa in Japan in the 1940s. It provides pictorial relationships between the many possible causes of a given effect.

The use of the diagram involves group brainstorming to create the listing of causes and group involvement in organizing the causes under the appropriate headings.

It is a powerful tool to bring the involved group into a consensus of causes and support their establishing a meaningful priority to pursue solution of the "effect."

The process is described in *Guide to Quality Control,* by Kaoru Ishikawa (Tokyo: Asian Productivity Organization, 1976).

Cause-and-Effect Diagram with Cards (CEDAC)

An adaptation of the original Ishikawa diagram for promoting a higher level of involvement and ownership.

This process first develops a basic cause-and-effect diagram (Ishikawa diagram). It uses the freedom to add information on a continuous basis as a key difference. The result is a "living" diagram that is continuously changing, not waiting for an update at a monthly or weekly meeting.

Managerial Engineering, by Ryuji Fukuda (Stamford, Conn.: Productivity, Inc., 1983), provides details on the application of this process plus other key management techniques, such as stockless production (JIT).

Design of Experiments

A process for optimizing a design or set of manufacturing variables using the least number of experiments.

This technique of fractional factorial statistics allows a process with many variables to be analyzed for the optimum combination in one third or less of the tests otherwise needed. The benefits are cost savings on experimental runs and the optimization of the process with high accuracy as compared to traditional guesswork techniques, or 100 percent testing of all variable combinations.

Two resources, both excellent, include Douglas C. Montgomery's book,

Design and Analysis of Experiments (New York: John Wiley & Sons, 1976) and the Process Management Institute (7801 East Bush Lake Road, Bloomington, Minn. 55435).

Job Content Analysis

In this process a statistical technique is used to sample what a person does and to provide data on how time is really spent. This data then allows analysis of the tasks to determine if they are being done by the right person or even in the right department.

The Extensor System of professional and management level work measurement was invented in Sweden and developed in the United States. Its extensive use by organizations and individuals has helped optimize job cost definitions using the least amount of time and work interruption. The system is applicable to a wide variety of job types where the employee makes decisions regarding how the job sequence and content are managed. For training/consulting contact Dr. John Robertson of The Extensor Corporation, 17273 Hampton Court, Minnetonka, Minn. 55345).

Just-in-Time (JIT)

A process leading to stockless production where needed materials arrive at an operation "just in time."

The benefits of a JIT system are significant:

1. Reduced work in process (WIP).
2. Reduced salvage or scrap when a fault is identified (few parts to scrap).
3. Quick identification of faulty product when it doesn't work at the next operation (minutes later).
4. Higher product quality. Few products include parts not meeting requirements.
5. Reduced inventory costs.
6. Shorter lead time to make changes.

See Richard J. Schoenberger's book, *Japanese Manufacturing Techniques* (New York: Free Press, 1982), and *Kanban: Just in Time at Toyota* by the Japan Management Association (Cambridge, Mass.: Productivity Press, 1986).

Profit Sharing/Gain Sharing

Two terms that are frequently used interchangeably. However, they are different.

Profit Sharing is a process that shares with employees some specified amount or percentage of profits. It provides a sense of ownership through the sharing process. It lacks a feeling of control since the profit is a function of both employee efficiency and market determination of price. They can't control price and, therefore, can't really control profit.

Gain Sharing is a process that measures gains in productivity caused by employee-identified changes in labor or material used. The gain sharing concept can be applied to small work groups and reinforce team or circle reviews of the process. It is applicable to office, service, or manufacturing. It is easy to establish ownership and measure the impact of what a group of employees accomplished. It shares a percent of the dollars saved either to each small work group or as an average to a whole company. An excellent process with circles and reinforces use of statistics or other techniques of problem solving. It ties directly to a suggestion system.

There are numerous books on profit sharing, gain sharing, scanlon plans, or contact the Profit Sharing Research Foundation (1718 Sherman Avenue, Evanston, Ill. 60201).

Quality of Work Life (QWL)

The recognition of job satisfaction as a basis for employee productivity is summarized in the concept of quality of work life. This concept relates the needs of all employees for dignity, a feeling of self-worth, and ownership, in addition to a clean, safe work place and assurance of continued employment.

A field of study and application for QWL has emerged as socio-technical systems where the needs of the person and those of technology can be effectively brought together.

Eric Trist is considered the first researcher based on studies in Europe after World War II. He has extensive publications along with numerous other authors.

Another source for material is the Ontario Quality of Working Life Centre (400 University Avenue, Toronto, Ontario, Canada M7A-1T7).

Single Minute Exchange of Dies (SMED)

A concept of tooling design allowing rapid changeover from one piece part to another and allowing very small economical runs.

SMED identifies concepts that standardize variations in die size and its location such that change can be made without adjustments to the machine and with a minimum of work or special fixtures.

This concept is applicable to all types of machinery (lathes, punch press, plastic mold, etc.).

The SMED concept is fundamental to accomplishing JIT or stockless production. Rapid tooling change supports economic production of small lots and helps reduce scrap and salvage costs. See A Revolution in Manufacturing — The SMED System, by Shigeo Shingo (Productivity, Inc., 1985).

Statistical Process Control (SPC) and Statistical Quality Control (SQC)

The use of statistical methods to track process variance (changes) or to predict the capability of a process to meet specifications.

The process uses a wide range of statistical techniques ranging from simple to complex. Most organizations will be able to effect improvements using the simple techniques.

Statistics allow data to be presented in a visual or graphic style allowing easy understanding of how well a given process is working.

The process is applicable to identifying quality of a product in either office or factory.

A parallel process, statistical quality control (SQC), uses the same methods and is usually seen as identical. Some view that the SQC concentrates on measurement of product variance while SPC tries to prevent product variance.

A large number of sources for training exist. Those I have experience with include: Process Management Institute (Suite 360, 7801 East Bush Lake Road, Bloomington, Minn. 55435); W. Edwards Deming (George Washington University); and Transformation of American Industry, Productivity Quality Associates, Inc. (P.O. Box 633, Dayton, Ohio 45459).

Suggestion System

A structured process to encourage employees or customers to submit ideas for improvement.

The system can either solicit "problems" or solicit "problems and a suggested solution." Some systems allow either method to be used.

Systems formalize the process and require a written response to each idea. Savings can be calculated and cash or other awards granted based on savings.

Suggestion systems are effective as a separate program or operated in conjunction with quality circles and task teams.

Details are available from the National Association of Suggestion Systems and Total Quality Systems (465 W. Eagle Lake Drive, Maple Grove, Minn. 55369).

William Tracey's book, *Human Resources Management and Development Handbook* contains details on suggestion systems and other processes.

Total Quality Control (TQC)

A concept that causes all employees to be involved in creating quality product. Product is defined as what you produce and pass to another person. This means lathe operators, assemblers, secretaries, managers, engineers, etc., all monitor the quality of what they produce and attempt to achieve zero defects (memos, designs, parts, etc.).

This process is based on everyone having responsibility for the quality of their work. Current traditional processes use a quality control function to find errors (detection) and help identify methods for prevention.

The concept appears simple but it really reflects a major change in the attitudes, responsibilities, and ownership of all employees. The concept will cause changes in responsibility and job content. The result is a large reduction in errors made and resulting cost savings in labor and material. The following books are good sources of information: *Japanese Manufacturing Techniques,* by Richard J. Schonberger (New York: Free Press, 1982); and *What Is Total Quality Control,* by Kaoru Ishikawa, translated by David J. Lu (Englewood Cliffs, N.J.: Prentice-Hall, Inc., 1985).

Value Engineering/Value Analysis (VE/VA)

Originally used in the review of product designs either before production release or even after several years of manufacture. The process is a structured analytical process that supports analysis of all elements of a product leading to improvements in quality, cost, and operation.

The process is being renamed value analysis to support the broadened use of the methods. Significant improvements using VA have been made in merchandising, office, hospital, and other service industries.

The process was initiated in the United States many years ago. The largest users are in Japan, where it is recognized as a powerful tool. Training is available from Professional Value Services (2000 Aldrich Avenue South, Minneapolis, Minn. 55405) and the Society of American Value Engineers (SAVE).

Work Simplification/Work Flow Analysis (WS/WFA)

A process to analyze the movement of a product through the cycle of its manufacture or processing.

The process of work simplification was used effectively during World War II. It was a key analysis tool used with teams or circles to do problem solving in the 1950s.

The process is widely used in Japan and Europe. It is frequently taught to teams training in statistical process control.

The process uses team involvement techniques developed by Allan Mogensen who provides two week seminars at his "Work Simplification Conferences." He can be reached at Work Simplification Conferences, P.O. Box 30, Lake Placid, N.Y. 12945.

Paperwork Simplification

An adaptation of Allan Mogensen's process to optimize the application to solving office paperwork problems.

Dr. Ben Graham, Jr., has created unique methods to analyze the actions involved in producing paperwork leading to simplification and work reduction, a necessary first step to automation of office paperwork. Write to Dr. Graham at 6600 South Troy-Frederick Road, Tipp City, Ohio 45371.

Zero Defects (ZD)

The concept originated in the 1950s to encourage quality as part of the military procurement process.

Zero defects is based on the fact that the costs of making errors or correcting faulty parts far exceed the costs to "do it right the first time." Also, that we cannot afford the costs of scrap and salvage and be competitive in world markets.

Philip B. Crosby is the recognized leader in this philosophy and has trained thousands of managers in the concept at his "Quality College" in Winter Park, Florida. He also wrote *Quality Is Free* (New York: McGraw-Hill Book Co., 1979).

The process involves a measurement of the "cost of nonquality" or the costs associated with making and correcting errors. This cost process then stimulates problem solving and error prevention. The process is applicable to service organizations as well as manufacturing.

References

Amsden, D.M., and R.T. Amsden. "Problems with Q.C. Circles." *Proceedings of the Second Annual IAQC Conference* in San Francisco. Midwest City, OK: International Association of Quality Circles, 1980.

Aubrey, C., and W. Fencel. "Management, Professional, and Clerical Quality Circles." *Transactions of the Thirty-Ninth Annual ASQC Technical Conference* in Detroit. Milwaukee: American Society for Quality Control, 1982.

Deming, W.E. *On the Management of Statistical Techniques for Quality and Productivity.* Washington, DC: W.E. Deming, 1981.

Francis, D. "QC Circles at Norfolk Naval Shipyard." Paper presented at the First Annual Dayton Quality Circles Seminar, Dayton, OH, 1980.

Friedlander, F., and L.D. Brown. "Organization Development." *Annual Review of Psychology* 25 (1974).

Goodfellow, M. "Supervisors: Key to Quality Control." *Telephone Engineer and Management Magazine* (15 May 1981): 71-74.

Gottschalk, E.C., Sr. "U.S. Firms Worried by Productivity Lag, Copy Japan in Seeking Employees' Advice." *Wall Street Journal* (21 February 1980): 40.

Ishikawa, K. *Basic Concepts of Company-Wide Quality Control and Status of Quality Circles Activities in Japan.* Japan: Japanese Union of Scientists and Engineers, 1981.

Juran, J.M. *Quality Control Handbook.* New York: McGraw-Hill, 1952.

Katzell, R.A., P. Bienstock, and P.H. Faerstein. *A Guide to Worker Productivity Experiments in the United States: 1971-1975.* Work in America Institute, Inc. New York: New York University Press, 1977.

Law, J.M. "Quality Circles Zero in on Productivity at the Norfolk Naval Shipyard." *Management* 1, No. 4 (1980): 2-5.

Leavitt, H.J. "Applied Organizational Change in Industry: Structural Technological and Humanistic Approaches." In *Handbook of Organizations,* edited by J.G. March. Chicago: Rand McNally, 1965.

Nelson, D.J. "What Motivated People Can Do." *Proceedings of the Second Annual IAQC Conference* in San Francisco. Midwest City, OK: International Association of Quality Circles, 1980.

Ouchi, W. *Theory Z.* Reading, MA: Addison-Wesley, 1981.

Patchin, R.I. "Quality Control Circles." Unpublished technical report. Los Angeles: January 1981.

Patchin, R.I. "Remarks on Quality Circles, Northrop's Experience." Unpublished transcript of testimony before the Congressional Subcommittee on Trade, Committee on Ways and Means, Washington, DC: October 1980.

Poza, E.J. "The New American Factory." *Productivity* 2 (March 1981): 1-4.

Rieker, W.S. "What Is the Lockheed Quality Control Circle Program?" *Transactions of the Thirtieth Annual ASQC Technical Conference* in Toronto. Milwaukee: American Society for Quality Control, 1976.

Schleicher, W.F. "Quality Control Circles Save Lockheed Nearly $3 Million in Two Years." *Quality* (May 1977): 4-17.

Sikes, W., J. Connell, and M.D. Donovan. "Learning from Experience." *Proceedings of the Second Annual IAQC Conference* in San Francisco. Midwest City, OK: International Association of Quality Circles, 1980.

"Stunning Turnaround at Tarrytown." *Time* (5 May 1980):87.